/

Prosperity Projects

Seven projects to prioritize your most urgent money decision.

Published by: Finn & Mav Press

Zaccary Call

Table of Contents

Zaccary Call

All That Matters

I'm proud of my Uber rating. I have no idea if passenger ratings are real or if drivers can see them. However, I am bent on preserving mine.

I imagine a scenario in which the rain is pouring hard during a family vacation in an unfamiliar city. I am convinced that I will be able to draw from my Uber bank account of karma. At that very moment, a five-star rating will entice a kind driver to accept my ride request.

To maintain my unknowable passenger rating, I always engage with my driver in conversation. My fascination for people and their personal financial situation leads me into deep conversations about my driver's life and money. I have learned if you ask, "What does the average person make around here?", you will hear exactly how much the driver makes. If you ask, "What do people pay for rent or mortgages?" or "How expensive are homes around here?", they will tell you their mortgage payment and home value.

When the driver finds out what I do for a living, he or she will almost always ask something like, "What stock should I buy?" or "I've been trading in crypto and what do you think about...?" Essentially, they ask me an investment related question.

It is not the wrong question; it is the *wrong time* to ask the question.

But to show the importance of the timing, let's pretend an Uber passenger tells a driver about a computer chip producer called NVIDIA. Our hypothetical is set in January 2010 and the driver decides to invest all $100,000 of his life's savings into the stock. If the Uber driver can hold on for a little over 14 years until June of 2024, he will finish with $29 million. Unfortunately, six months into the drive of life, the Uber driver gets sick and can't work. His family is in desperate need of cash the next month, so they sell his NVIDIA stock in August 2010, only seven months from purchase. The stock took a massive hit during that time, and he walked away with only $47,350, losing over half his value.

This stock has been one of the best performing stocks of all time. NVIDIA has made many millionaires. The results from a June 2024 twitter poll of over 3,000 NVIDIA employees (posted by @FilledWithMoney on Twitter) showed that over one third of the responding employees had wealth worth more than $20M. My goodness.

This example was extremely hypothetical, especially the luck needed to put all your money in the best performing stock 15 years in advance. However, it teaches us a valuable lesson. The driver was on track to have $29 million, but he walked away with only $47,350.

It didn't matter that this stock trade was so good it is the answer you would give when asked, "What would you do with a time machine?" All that mattered was that the Uber driver didn't have an emergency fund.

Important financial decisions were made in the wrong order. The order was all that mattered.

Even one of the best performing stocks of our lifetime couldn't save this financial household. Financial planning, if done *in the right order*, could have.

This is why I created the 7 Prosperity Projects. The projects do not make you rich. YOU will make you rich. I will show you the order in which to do it.

How to Start

Welcome to your guide to financial planning and savings decisions. This book is your roadmap, offering a step-by-step approach to building, and securing your financial future. If you are trying to build wealth before retirement, this guide will tell you what to do and in what order.

The methodology outlined in this book is not the only path to financial security, but it is a prudent approach. As a wealth advisor, I have had the privilege of analyzing the financial situations of thousands of households. This project-based financial security program mimics the strategies of the most successful households I have encountered. The steps provided here help you avoid taking on major financial risks by addressing the most critical tasks upfront.

As you progress, you will gradually build a solid foundation upon which you can construct lasting wealth structure. These projects take the guesswork out of the order in which you should tackle each financial task.

Each section of this book is a "project." These projects represent the key areas you should address simultaneously to achieve financial security. Each project contains several tasks. For some of the projects, the tasks are sequential. Meaning, address each task in a specific order. In other projects, the tasks are simultaneous. This means you should divide your financial resources and time between all the tasks within the project at the same time. As we approach each project, I will let you know which project is sequential or simultaneous.

The project order is the most important aspect of this book. You may decide to make minor adaptations to an individual task, wonderful. The point is that you are successful in your way. There will come a moment along your money decision path when you wonder if you are missing something. You may wonder if you are addressing something too early. The order of the 7 Prosperity Projects provides those answers.

Partners and Money

One of my best friends in high school and I played center midfield together on the soccer pitch. If you are less familiar with the game, teams often play two or even three people in the middle of the field given the amount of space to cover. The center-midfielders need to have a similar approach. If you crowd each other, you will clog up the passing lanes. If you are too far apart, passing options will not exist. My friend had one of the best work rates on the team. He would run toward the ball regardless of whether it was on the left or right side of the field. I knew we needed proper spacing, so I found myself adjusting to his movement. I spent entire games running away from the ball to counteract his movement towards it. We were as efficient as described by comedian, Brian Regan, when he acts befuddled about seeing two semitrucks passing each other on the highway while delivering the exact same type of logs to lumberyards on the opposite coasts. This is where the marriage bickering began. During practice we would argue about tactics. The coaches hoped we would work it out, but eventually they played me on the wing...we got divorced.

This happens often with money and couples. One spouse views money as a resource to create experiences. Another spouse may feel a large bank account is a security blanket and having the money is worth more than experiencing the money. For others, it is a scorecard or a game. Imagine being the spouse who likes the security blanket, and someone is pillaging your safety net for travel. Conversely, imagine you feel like your life is passing by too quickly and someone is hoarding the resources you need to live life optimally. Lastly, imagine you want to compete, you want to win, and you enjoy the process, however your spouse is unwilling to take any risks.

The point is not that anyone is right. The advice is that you need to do three things:

1. Figure out what money means to you.
2. Communicate your money values to your partner.
3. Most importantly, imagine what it is like to coordinate with someone who has your money

values, because your partner is not just imagining it, they are living it.

Some people are financially successful without good money communication between partners. Later, the less financially savvy partner often confesses to their advisor or therapist they are not happy. Your ability to talk openly about money with your partner is the only way to avoid trading your marriage for wealth.

Again, figure yourself out, communicate it, imagine how that feels for your partner. It is a good relationship recipe for any topic, but especially money values.

The 7 Prosperity Projects:

Project 1: Plug the Holes in the Boat

The first project focuses on emergency preparedness and risk management. It is hard to get anywhere on a ship that is leaking. You will learn how to create an emergency fund, address life's major uncertainties with appropriate insurance, and pay down high-interest debt. By taking care of these critical areas first, you lay the groundwork for a stable financial future.

Project 2: Get Free Money

Employer matching is often an immediate 100% return on your investment. Discover how to maximize employer benefits like HSA matching, retirement plan matching programs, and employee stock purchase plans. This project ensures you are not leaving any free money on the table.

Project 3: Optimize Retirement Plans and Tax Benefits

Once you have eliminated or insured against major risks and you are getting all the free money available to you, it is time to model out your retirement savings flight plan. In Project 3 you will do projections and determine the right savings rates. You will learn how to optimize your retirement savings by considering the tax structures of each of your retirement plan options. Lastly, you will assess your current and future tax situations so you can choose the right retirement accounts.

Project 4: Decide who is in Charge

You are starting to accumulate wealth and responsibilities. Project 4 is all about the process of outlining the instructions to protect the people and assets in your life. This process is estate planning. This project will help you ensure your family relationships stay strong and that your wishes are carried out if you die or become disabled.

Project 5: Reduce Unwanted Debt

Learn strategies to manage and reduce debt effectively. This project will guide you through the process of prioritizing and paying down debts to improve your financial health.

Project 6: Build Non-Retirement Wealth

Explore the benefits of investing outside of retirement accounts. From real estate to small businesses and standard brokerage accounts, this project emphasizes building wealth through diverse investment opportunities.

Project 7: Swing for the Fences

This final project encourages you to take calculated risks with potentially high rewards. You will learn how to identify and pursue investment opportunities that could significantly boost your wealth.

The primary purpose of these seven projects is to provide you with the financial decision-making order. We will describe these steps in enough detail that you will feel empowered to act. However, the greatest improvement to your money decision making will come from prioritizing the projects. Just like the best camera to take a picture is the one you are willing to carry with you, the best financial plan is the one you can implement. By following this guide, you will make informed decisions and confidently navigate your financial journey.

You will hear many differing opinions about the order of operations when it comes to financial planning. That does not mean that you are on the wrong path. Just like everyone was not meant to be an artist, not everyone is meant to follow the same financial journey. Some people swear by taking massive risks for growth. This is often the case for business founders who survived. Meaning, the founder started in Project 7 and experienced an elevated level of risk throughout their wealth creation journey. The wealthiest individuals I have ever met are business owners and founders. Building insane wealth is a different topic and one for another day, but it is not this list. This list is the prudent and predicable path to wealth. These seven projects will get you to financial security without ever placing you too close to the edge of a financial cliff. Whether you prioritize the slow and steady approach or dream bigger through business start-ups and exits, you should consider the prosperity projects. Even if you are trying to build a nest egg worth hundreds of millions of dollars, the 7 Prosperity Projects should at least be your plan B, and you should address them alongside your audacious goal.

It is time to take control of your financial future and build the security and wealth you deserve.

Before you jump into Project 1, I want to save you from potential heartache and frustration. Most games and sports have some level of both offense and defense. The financial game does as well. Between financial offense and defense, financial professionals often avoid discussing one. Let us embark on this journey together with a quick discussion about both financial offense and defense.

Zaccary Call

Financial Offense and Defense

In the journey towards financial independence and wealth building, understanding the balance between making money and managing money is crucial. This chapter, "Financial Offense and Defense," will explore these two essential aspects of income management, setting the stage for the detailed projects that follow.

Financial Defense: The B-word (Budgeting)

Your ability to manage the dollars passing through your bank account is what I call "financial defense." It is hard.

It requires systems and willpower. For some people, the word "budgeting" is loaded with emotion, and it means marriage arguments. If you feel that way, you are not alone. Only a few strange people enjoy tracking expenses, and their spouse or partner rarely feels the same. I am convinced these people are the same ones who have convinced themselves they love running marathons. It seems a bit like an "Emperor's New Clothes" situation.

An alternative to budgeting is automation. Regardless of how we may feel about the b-word, you need a method of controlling your burn rate. This ensures that you make the most out of the money you earn. Will power is a muscle that fatigues easily. Rather than require your own mental muscle to fight urge and impulse, use automation. Make automatic transfers to a spending account. Only spend the money in that spending account. I call that the "Fake Paycheck" method. Make automatic savings transfers. Fund important goals first. You have heard all this before as "pay yourself first" and financial "experts" have overdone this topic.

I have learned a lot about systems from James Clear's book "Atomic Habits." He said, "I've found that goals are good for *planning* your progress and systems are good for actually *making* progress." We all have a goal of managing our cashflow better, but how many of us change our system to make progress? The secret is to design your systems to make progress effortless.

Key Components of Financial Defense:

1. **Know your burn rate:** In the beginning, it is not about making perfect money decisions. It is about at least knowing what decisions you are making. Many of us avoid looking because it is embarrassing and painful. Do it alone first if you must.

2. **Automate the good, restrict the bad:** Determine the outcomes you desire. Set up automatic transfers and payments that require effort to stop. Sometimes it is easier to let an auto-transfer happen than to stop it. Speaking of friction, put friction in front of your undesirable behaviors. If seeing your emergency fund tempts you to spend it, move it to another financial institution introducing friction (transfers and clearing time) to move the funds to a spendable position.

Financial Defense has limits. At some point you have saved all your income leaving you with nothing for essentials. This is the same as producing a defensive shutout in a soccer match. You cannot win the game without scoring a goal. Financial experts often ignore Financial Offense. No one wants to tell you that you are not earning enough money, but sometimes it is true.

Financial Offense: The Power of Earning

Think of financial offense as your ability to generate income. Just as a sports team needs a strong offense to score points, you may need to increase your income to build wealth. While frugality and careful spending are essential, they can only take you so far. Not having enough income limits your ability to save and invest.

I coach competitive youth soccer. There have been times when I was worried about locking down the opponent's attack, so I adjusted the formation or moved my star players to defensive positions to individually mark (follow) their best players. This can backfire. The best defense is a relentless attack. It is hard to give up a goal when you are on the attack in their half of the field.

I am not insinuating that people should be irresponsible with their spending or financial defense. You still want a goalie in the goal and talented defenders. I am telling you to not beat yourself up emotionally for conceding goals, especially if you are not playing enough financial offense. You cannot budget your way to wealth if every dollar is spoken for by essential expenses. A weak financial offense may be the reason you are giving up goals on defense.

Imagine losing $10,000 on an investment. Painful right? Now imagine the luxury of having an extra $25,000 of income every month after your bills are paid. Well, that is different. That is like going down one goal in the beginning of a soccer match and having Lionel Messi as your forward. He is the most creative offensive player in the world today in 2024. My kids often play a "would you rather" game in which they ask you to pick between two undesirable situations. If they asked, "would you rather start every match down 0-1 with Messi or 0-0 without him?" I would pick Messi every time. It is the same with finances. Would you rather start with:

- $50,000 of debt, making $300,000 per year, or
- $50,000 in savings, making $80,000 per year

It seems easy to pick $300,000 when you put it in this perspective, but it is not so simple. A change in offense (your job, your time, your focus) often means real changes to our lives.

How to know if you are playing enough financial offense:

This is a "feel" thing, but there are some ways to know if you are in the ballpark. First, Google the average cost of living in your state or your area and second, multiply it by these factors:

- 1/2 for general happiness
- 1/4 for each child you have
- 1/3 for wealth building capacity

Lastly, add those three values to the average cost of living in your state.

For example, if the average cost of living in your area is $60,000 and you have two children:

- 1/2 X $60,000 = $30,000 (happiness factor)
- 1/4 X $60,000 X 2 kids = $30,000 (child factor)
- 1/3 X $60,000 = $20,000 (wealth building factor)

Your minimum financial offense in this scenario is $140,000.

You should try to earn $60,000 + $30,000 (happiness factor) + $30,000 (2 children, $15,000 each) + $20,000 (wealth building capacity) = $140,000

If your income exceeds this formula and you still find it difficult to make progress towards financial security, you should spend time improving your financial defense.

Strategies for Strengthening Your Financial Offense:

1. **Invest in Education:** Higher education and specialized training can open doors to better-paying job opportunities. Consider certifications, online courses, or advanced degrees that align with your career goals. Spending $5,000 on specialized training that will help you earn an extra $2,000 per month is much better than putting $5,000 into a Roth IRA.

2. **Seek Promotions:** Aim for career advancement within your current job. Take on additional responsibilities, demonstrate leadership, and make your aspirations known to your

supervisors. Your supervisor is busy; politely ensure your manager is considering your wellbeing and contributions. I try to be aware of my team members' career paths, however, I have also needed a reminder from them from time to time as other urgent items have occupied my attention. However, I have welcomed those conversations to ensure I am fair and to avoid the employees feeling like they need to resort to changing jobs.

3. **Change Jobs:** Sometimes, the best way to increase your income is to switch employers. Research shows that job-hoppers often see higher salary increases compared to those who stay with one employer for extended periods. This can backfire. Depending on your profession, you may benefit from building up a practice or book of business. Also, changing jobs too frequently may reflect poorly on your resume.

4. **Start a Side Hustle:** Leverage your skills and passions to create additional income streams. Whether it is freelancing, consulting, or starting a small business, a side hustle can significantly boost your earning potential.

I have not listed income producing properties, dividends, or other investments as financial offense. Financial offense is the cashflow that comes from your time. Long-term investing is another game entirely. We will get to that. Your efforts to bring in new cashflow, your offense, allows you to invest. Your investments protect your wealth against inflation and after a while can add to your financial offense.

Balancing Offense and Defense

The key to winning the money game is to strike a balance between financial offense and defense. While you need to generate a sufficient income to support your financial goals, you also need to manage that income wisely.

1. **Set Clear Goals:** Establish short-term and long-term financial goals. Knowing what you are working towards can motivate you to earn more and spend wisely.

2. **Automate Success:** You can use brute force, or you can become wealthy effortlessly. The difference is in the level of automation you implement.

3. **Regularly Review Your Finances:** Periodic reviews of your income, expenses, and savings help you stay on track. Adjust your strategies as needed to ensure you are making progress towards your goals.

4. **Stay Flexible:** Life is unpredictable, and your financial situation may change. Be prepared to adapt your offense and defense as needed.

The Path Forward

As you embark on the journey through the 7 projects outlined in this book, keep the concepts of financial offense and defense in mind. Each project will build upon these foundational principles, helping you create a comprehensive financial plan.

Remember, the purpose of this book is to provide you with the order to address each financial decision and enough instructions so you can act. By understanding and implementing both offensive and defensive financial strategies, you will have the money to navigate the complexities of financial planning and achieve financial independence.

7 Prosperity Projects

You may decide to act immediately as you learn the details in each project. There is a worksheet at the end of this book that you may use to keep track of your progress and take notes. Imagine your financial ship is sinking. This is where we begin Project 1.

Zaccary Call

Prosperity Project 1: Plug the Holes in the Boat

You need to ensure your financial vessel is seaworthy. This means addressing any immediate vulnerabilities that could jeopardize your financial well-being. In this chapter, we will focus on the first critical project: "Plug the holes in the boat." This involves three essential tasks: creating an emergency fund, solving for "the big what ifs" with insurance, and paying down high-interest debt.

Project 1 contains simultaneous tasks. You should not wait until you have all your high-interest debt paid off and a large emergency fund before you sign up for life insurance. What if you pass away before that point?

Dedicate your time and your resources to all three tasks right away. When a project contains simultaneous tasks, we will use letters A, B, C, and so on. When it contains sequential tasks, we will use numbers 1, 2, 3, and so on.

Task A: Create an Emergency Fund

An emergency fund is your first line of defense against unexpected financial setbacks. It acts as a buffer that allows you to cover unforeseen expenses without derailing your long-term financial plans. The appropriate amount for an emergency fund varies based on your income stability, risk tolerance, and family dynamics.

Determining the Right Amount

1. **Income Stability:** If you have a stable, dual-income household, a general rule is to have three months' worth of expenses saved in your emergency fund. This is because the likelihood of losing both incomes simultaneously is lower. For single-income households, it is prudent to increase this buffer to six months' worth of

expenses, as the consequence is greater if you lose that sole income.

2. **Risk Tolerance:** If you have a lower risk tolerance, you may feel more comfortable with a larger safety net. Conversely, if you have no children, are confident in your ability to quickly find new employment, or have other sources of income, you might opt for a smaller fund.

3. **Family Dynamics:** Consider your personal and family circumstances. If you have children, you might need a larger fund to cover potential emergencies.

Steps to Build Your Emergency Fund

1. **Calculate Your Monthly Expenses:** You could list all your monthly expenses, including housing, utilities, groceries, transportation, insurance, and other essentials. If you find this difficult or daunting, do not let that stop you. Instead, look at your paycheck. If you receive X amount every two weeks, use that as your "expenses." It is not perfect, but it is going to be close, and it is better than taking no action.

2. **Set a Savings Goal**: Based on your household type and risk tolerance, determine the target amount for your emergency fund (e.g., three or six months of expenses).

3. **Create a Savings Plan**: Decide how much you can realistically save each month and set up automatic transfers to a separate savings account dedicated to your emergency fund. Do not allocate every dollar of income to this. You will need some of your extra income for Task B and Task C.

4. **Adjust as Needed**: Periodically review and adjust your emergency fund to ensure it remains adequate for your changing circumstances.

Task B: Solve for "The Big What Ifs"

Life is unpredictable, and having the right insurance coverage can protect you and your family from significant financial hardship in case of major life events like death or disability.

Life Insurance

1. **Determine Your Coverage Needs**: Consider factors such as your income, debt, living expenses, and future financial goals (e.g., children's education). A common guideline is to have coverage that is 10-12 times your annual income. This is a start, but not enough to fully cover your family. Keep in mind that we are only plugging holes in the boat, not making the perfect ship. You can add more life insurance later if needed. If you want to get closer to solving your entire life insurance need, do 20-25 times your income now.

2. **Choose the Right Policy**: There are several types of life insurance policies, including term life and whole life. Term life insurance is affordable and straightforward. It is in place for a specific period. I prefer it in nearly every scenario. I lost my life insurance through an employment change. While at this employer, I experienced a cancer diagnosis. New life insurance is off the table for me because insurance carriers won't accept this health event on my record. It is beneficial to have term life

insurance separate from your employer offered plan so you can keep it no matter where you work.

3. **Review and Update Regularly**: Life insurance needs can change over time, so review your policy periodically and update it as necessary to ensure it meets your current needs.

Disability Insurance

1. **Understand the Importance**: Disability insurance replaces a portion of your income if you become unable to work due to illness or injury. Disability insurance is important because the risk of becoming disabled during your working years is higher than most workers realize.
2. **Assess Employer Coverage**: Check if your employer offers disability insurance and understand the terms and coverage limits.
3. **Supplement if Necessary**: If your employer's coverage is insufficient, consider purchasing an individual policy to fill the gaps.
4. **Separate Coverage from Your Employer**: You may want to have a separate policy from your

employer that can move along with you if you choose to change jobs. Your employer often subsidizes the employer offered option which makes it less expensive for you.

Guardianship

- **Discuss with your spouse/partner:** Step one is to discuss the possible successor guardians for your children. If you and your spouse or partner pass away without guardianship instructions organized, a judge will make the decisions about who will raise your minor children.

- **Consider environment and values:** Your primary consideration should be to place your children with safe parents who share similar values and beliefs with you. You will need to ensure these new parents will love your children as their own.

- **Consider non-financial capability:** Even if your appointed guardian shares your values and loves your children, you may need to choose someone else if this person has too many other time commitments or obligations. If they already have five kids, adding your four might be the wrong environment.

- **Consider financial capability:** Your life insurance proceeds should help, but it is important that adding your children does not place the existing family in too much of a financial constraint. The family may comingle assets and income. Meaning your money that is dedicated to just your kids may be mixed with the rest of the new guardian's assets just as your kids would be integrated into the family social dynamic. I am not convinced this is an improper thing even though many estate planners will try to protect against it. I would want the guardians to consider my children to be the same as their own biological children in every sense. The lesson is to be mindful of the social dynamics of having wealthy kids living with less wealthy parents and siblings.

I know a family that had no assets. For that reason, they did not do any estate planning. The mother and father died in an accident. After the young couple passed, the children became the center of a difficult legal battle as several parties believed they should be the new caretakers. Guardianship instructions are both important and urgent even if you feel like you don't have much of a financial estate. There are some attorneys that will help you with one or two simple documents rather than charging for an entire estate plan. This is a good way to establish a temporary solution until you have more time and money to build your comprehensive foundational estate plan.

Liability Insurance

1. **Home insurance:** Do not let a house fire or other event wipe out your emergency fund or worse, lose your home.
2. **Car insurance:** Your deductibles and coverage amounts should be high enough to cover the other party's medical bills and the cost of a brand-new vehicle.
3. **Umbrella insurance:** An umbrella policy coordinates with your standard liability coverage and covers additional liability. It is overkill for someone with minimal assets and responsibilities, however, I know millionaires are also reading this book — how else do you think they became millionaires, but by learning about money? — so additional liability coverage is worth it. Do some research and put this inexpensive policy in place.
4. **Professional liability insurance:** Do not let a mistake in your professional life destroy your personal wealth. The right legal structures are

important to protect you, but in some cases, you should also have liability coverage. Examples are a doctor, lawyer, or any profession with a high probability of being sued for a mistake or malpractice.

Task C: Pay Down High-Interest Debt

High-interest debt can be a significant drain on your financial resources, making it harder to achieve your financial goals. Paying down this debt should be a top priority. Sometimes it is hard to know exactly what percentage rate "high interest" debt is. When home rates are low as 3% or high as 7%, I still consider anything with a double-digit interest rate to be "high interest". If rates are down near 3% for a 30-year fixed rate, you might even consider 7% to be "high-interest". However, we are being a bit nitpicky. The destructive high-interest debt is often credit card debt and it is often near 20% for the annual interest rate. You will not make it to prosperity keeping 20% credit card debt. Pay it off. Get another job if you must. This debt is not just numerical, it will affect your relationships and your health.

Strategies for Debt Reduction

1. **List Your Debts**: Make a list of all your debts, including the balance, interest rate, and minimum monthly payment for each.

2. **Choose a Debt Reduction Method**: Two popular methods are the debt avalanche and the debt snowball:

   ○ **Debt Avalanche**: Focus on paying off the debt with the highest interest rate first while making minimum payments on the others. This method saves you the most money in interest payments over time.

   ○ **Debt Snowball**: Focus on paying off the smallest debt first while making minimum payments on the others. This method can provide psychological motivation by quickly eliminating smaller-balance debts.

3. **Increase Your Payments**: Allocate as much extra money as possible towards your chosen debt. This will absolutely mean cutting back on non-

essential expenses or finding additional sources of income. It may also mean cutting back on expenses you thought were essential. You do not climb out of debt without grit. Can you muster up enough?

4. **Monitor Your Progress**: Regularly track your progress and adjust your plan as necessary to stay on course.

Prosperity Project 1 Wrap Up

This recent summer, my wife Michelle, our three children, and I were on vacation walking through Amsterdam which is also known as "the city of bicycles". This was our first time in Amsterdam. If you have never seen the transportation system in Amsterdam, imagine the Atari game "Frogger" or if you are younger than about 40, imagine the "Crossy Road" app. The lanes go as follows: pedestrians, bicycles, vehicles, median (for stranded pedestrians), surface trams, vehicles, bicycles, and finally...the other pedestrian sidewalk. Somehow you must cross all these lanes, but not always at the same time.

Due to a brain tumor, Michelle is deaf in her left ear. She has no way to determine the direction of sound given that she only has one reference point, one working ear. She started to walk across the bicycle lane at an intersection. A cyclist was turning onto this street from behind us. The two were on a collision course. I blurted out a noise that meant nothing in any language, but it was effective. She halted and the collision was avoided. My teenagers still mock me to this day for that unearthly noise, but we really didn't have time to discuss the best way to alert her to the danger.

Prosperity project 1 may feel a bit blunt, however, right now there is no time to check in on how you feel about money and planning. I love Michelle dearly, but I screamed at her to keep her out of danger. Project 1 is a bit the same. These are direct and urgent instructions to prevent a financial collision.

By completing these three tasks…

- Creating an emergency fund
- Securing adequate insurance
- Paying down high-interest debt

...you are effectively "plugging the holes in the boat." These steps provide a solid foundation for your financial health, allowing you to weather storms and navigate towards your long-term financial goals with confidence.

At the end of each chapter, I will provide you with a checklist so you can mark your progress. A complete checklist is available at the end of the book. Remember, tasks with letters should be tackled simultaneously. Tasks with numbers are to be done in that order. Prosperity Project 1 is built with letters.

Prosperity Project 1 Checklist

- ☐ Task A: Create an Emergency Fund
  - ○ Determining the Right Amount
  - ○ Steps to Build Your Emergency Fund
- ☐ Task B: Solve for "The Big What Ifs"
  - ○ Life Insurance
  - ○ Disability Insurance
  - ○ Guardianship
  - ○ Liability Insurance
- ☐ Task C: Pay Down High-Interest Debt

In the next chapter, we will build on this solid foundation with something everyone loves: FREE MONEY!

Zaccary Call

Prosperity Project 2: Get Free Money

In Project 2, we explore how to take advantage of opportunities where you can receive "free money" through various employer-provided benefits. This project includes three key tasks: HSA matching, retirement plan matching, and employee stock purchase plans. If you understand and use these benefits, you can significantly enhance your financial well-being with minimal effort.

Project 2 contains sequential tasks. Remember that this means you will tackle each task in this very specific order. The tasks build upon each other. To help you remember when you are working on sequential tasks, the tasks are given numbers instead of letters.

Some people will recommend getting free money before paying down high-interest debt. I can see why. Mathematically, it is better in year one. For example, Jeff makes $200,000 per year and can set aside 5% of it to better improve his financial situation. That will be $10,000. Jeff can get a 5% match or avoid paying 20% interest on his credit card. Which is mathematically better?

If Jeff puts that money toward paying down credit card debt that charges 20% interest, he will save $2,000 of interest each year. That is amazing!

Jeff's 5% match is not just 5% of the $10,000, it is a 100% match of 5% of his income. If he allocates it to his 401(k) with a 100% match, he will make $10,000.

The credit card saves him (makes him) $2,000. The 401(k) makes him $10,000. Yet I am still saying that Jeff needs to forego the $10,000 match and allocate his $10,000 to his credit card debt.

Money issues are a result of bad money beliefs and behaviors. More money only amplifies the issues. Better money beliefs and behaviors eliminate them. Until Jeff learns how to handle having cash and being on the positive side of interest payments, he does not need the match as much as he needs the right structure.

Let's assume Jeff decides to contribute to the 401(k) instead of paying down the $10,000 of debt. The math in year two and beyond on the 401(k) contributions from year one is very different. Jeff is not getting a match in year two on the year-one contributions. Jeff has $20,000 in his 401k from year-one contributions, but he still has that $10,000 of debt. He must earn a 10% return in year two to break even with the $2,000 of debt interest he still had to pay on the debt. Markets often perform that well, but one of those rates is guaranteed (debt) and the other is just a possibility (investment).

Enough about interest, credit cards, matching, and math. The bottom line is this: You must build the beliefs and behaviors that prevent high interest debt. If you cannot manage spending and savings in a way to eliminate credit card debt, you must return to financial offense vs financial defense, automation, and behavior management. Even if there is free money, it does not help if it slides through your fingers. The good news is that anyone, at any moment, can adjust their money beliefs and build new behaviors. The knowledge from the rest of this book is going to help you.

Not everyone will have access to free money. Not everyone has an employer. If your employer does not offer you one of these plans, that is okay, move on to the next plan.

Task 1: HSA Matching

A Health Savings Account (HSA) is a powerful financial tool with triple tax benefits: contributions are tax-deductible, the account grows tax-free, and withdrawals for qualified medical expenses are tax-free. If your employer offers HSA matching, this is an excellent opportunity to maximize your savings.

Steps to Take:

1. **Understand Your HSA Plan:** Review the details of your employer's HSA plan. Determine the contribution limits for your plan. The contribution limit changes each year. Google "HSA contribution limit" to find today's limits. There are different limits for those whose health

plan covers a single individual vs a family, and still different limits for those over a certain age due to the ability to make additional catch-up contributions.

2. **Maximize Employer Contributions:** Find out how much your employer will match. This information is typically available in your benefits handbook or by contacting HR. Contribute at least enough to your HSA to get the full employer match. For example, if your employer matches up to $1,000, make sure you contribute at least $1,000 to receive the full benefit. The IRS contributions must include the match. For example, if the overall limit was $7,000 and your employer contributes $1,000. You can contribute an additional $6,000. Keep in mind that this is different from how the matching and max contribution limits work for a 401(k), 403(b), or other qualified plans.

3. **Automate Contributions:** Set up automatic payroll deductions to your HSA to ensure consistent contributions and to take full advantage of tax savings.

4. **Invest Your HSA Funds:** Consider investing your HSA funds if your plan allows it. Many HSA accounts offer investment options like retirement accounts, allowing your funds to grow over time. Most HSAs sit in cash earning little for the owner. Without investing, you are missing the tax-free growth benefit.

By prioritizing HSA contributions, you not only save on taxes but also build a fund for future medical expenses, reducing financial stress.

HSA Pro Tip: You can reimburse yourself for previous years' medical expenses. Knowing this allows for banking your medical expenses. You save the receipts for medical expenses and do not reimburse yourself immediately. That leaves your money to grow tax free within your HSA. You can reimburse yourself in the future at any time. A friendly suggestion: before you withdraw $20,000 worth of medical expense reimbursements in the future to pay for a family vacation or something else, double check that this strategy is still allowed.

Task 2: Retirement Plan Matching

Retirement plan matching, such as 401(k) and 403(b) programs, offers a significant benefit: a dollar-for-dollar match on a portion of your income, representing an immediate 50%-100% return on your contributions.

Steps to Take:

1. **Understand Your Retirement Plan:** Review the details of your employer's retirement plan, including the match percentage and contribution limits. The contribution limits are quite high for a 401(k)-plan relative to other retirement plan options. Those aged 50 or older can make additional catch-up contributions.

2. **Maximize Employer Match:** Contribute at least enough to your retirement plan to get the full employer match. For instance, if your employer matches 100% of the first 5% of your salary, ensure you contribute at least 5%. Another common plan offering is when your employer matches dollar-for-dollar on 3% and 50 cents on the dollar for the next 2%, ensure you contribute

at least 5% and your match will be 4% of your income.

3. **Automate Contributions:** Set up automatic payroll deductions to your retirement account to ensure consistent contributions and to capture the full employer match. Payroll contributions are typically the only way to contribute to a 401(k) plan.

4. **Review and Adjust Contributions Annually:** As your salary increases or your financial situation changes, consider increasing your contributions to maximize tax-free or tax-deferred growth.

5. **Diversify Your Investments:** Review your investment options within the retirement plan and diversify your portfolio to balance risk and return.

Maximizing your retirement plan match is one of the most effective ways to build long-term wealth and ensure a comfortable retirement.

Task 3: Employee Stock Purchase Plans (ESPP)

Employee Stock Purchase Plans (ESPP) allow you to buy company stock at a discount, often 10-15% below market price. This discount is free money and can provide a short-term gain even if you sell the stock immediately. These plans are less common than an HSA or 401(k). Only some employers offer ESPPs to their employees and most that do offer one are publicly traded companies. I would invest in an ESPP even if I did not plan to hold the stock long term. Some people will say, "but the taxes are worse if I sell it in the short term." This is true, but if you and I played a game in which if you give me $85 dollars, I immediately hand you $100 back and then you give $5 to the IRS? You get to keep $10 every time we play the game. Want to play again? This is your ESPP. If you are worried about the prospects of owning your stock for a brief period, I might also ask if you are worried about your job that is also subject to your employer's health.

Steps to Take:

1. **Understand Your ESPP:** Review the details of your employer's ESPP, including the discount rate, purchase periods, and holding requirements.

2. **Enroll in the ESPP:** Sign up for the ESPP during the enrollment period, usually offered a few times a year.

3. **Maximize Contributions:** Contribute as much as you can afford, up to the plan's maximum limit. The IRS has limits for ESPP contributions per year.

4. **Plan Your Strategy:** Decide whether to hold or sell the stock immediately. Selling immediately locks in the discount as a guaranteed gain. Holding the stock can potentially offer a lower tax rate and greater returns, but it comes with market risk.

5. **Monitor Your Holdings:** Keep track of your stock holdings and market performance. Diversify if your company stock represents a sizable portion of your portfolio to mitigate risk. At some point, you may have your current income, stock

options, ESPP, health care plan, and more all tied up with your employer. It can be prudent to diversify some of that risk by selling ESPP shares and buying other companies.

Utilizing your ESPP allows you to benefit from your company's growth while receiving an immediate financial boost from the purchase discount.

Prosperity Project 2 Wrap Up

Get Free Money is all about leveraging employer-provided benefits to maximize your financial gain with minimal effort. By taking advantage of HSA matching, retirement plan matching, and ESPP, you can significantly boost your savings and investments. Remember, the key to financial success is to understand and utilize these benefits effectively, ensuring you make the most of the opportunities available to you.

Prosperity Project 2 Checklist

- ☐ Task 1: HSA Matching
- ☐ Task 2: Retirement Plan Matching
- ☐ Task 3: Employee Stock Purchase Plans (ESPP)

Get ready for Project 3. By the end, you will have your savings target. I will make it easy, or at least easier, for you to understand one of the most complicated parts of retirement planning: predicting the future.

Prosperity Project 3: Automate Retirement Savings

This Prosperity Project is the most technical but try not to be intimidated. I will give you easy rules of thumb along the way.

Before we begin, if you are knocking out the prosperity projects as you work through this book, pause for a moment to admire your progress! You have plugged the holes in the boat, and you have started saving for retirement with your free money options. Congratulations!

If you are like me and you like to see the whole picture, you may have continued reading even if you are not finishing the projects as you read. Either way, imagine yourself having finished Project 2. You are safer and more protected. You are prepared to move on from financial danger and begin the process of building wealth.

This project seems complicated, but it does not have to be. You are trying to do two things:

1. Determine how much to save.
2. Determine to which account to contribute.

This can involve a lot of math factoring in growth and inflation, but it does not have to be complicated.

Project 3 contains sequential tasks. Remember that this means you will tackle each task in this very specific order. The tasks build upon each other. To help you remember when you are working on sequential tasks, the tasks are given numbers instead of letters.

This chapter will guide you through the six essential tasks to ensure you maximize your retirement savings while minimizing your tax burden. A few minor changes today will have a major impact on your retirement readiness. Let's begin.

Task 1: Determine How Much Money You Need to Save to Hit Your Retirement Goal

There is a significant difference in how precise your projections need to be for a 25-year-old hoping to retire in 35 to 40 years vs a 55-year-old who is starting to allocate specific dollars to spend in the early years of retirement. The younger you are, the less you should worry about every number. Just be directionally correct and revisit your estimates in the future.

The first step in optimizing your retirement plan is to determine your retirement spending goal. Ask yourself how much money you need to retire comfortably. This involves estimating your future expenses, including housing, healthcare, travel, and any other lifestyle choices you wish to maintain. Consider potential changes in your lifestyle, like a mortgage being paid off.

Steps to Determine Your Retirement Goal:

I am going to walk you through a simple table that will tell you how much to save. That is method 1. Method 2 is more mathematical. As your wealth gets more sophisticated you may want to run more precise calculations, however, this table will help you be directionally correct. You will find value in using "directionally correct" as a financial planning mentality. You need to be directionally correct and willing to adapt. A directionally-correct approach is much more successful than trying to be perfectly correct and unwilling to adapt. One approach encourages action and progress. The other discourages action because it requires perfection.

Method 1: The Easy Table.

Estimate how much you have saved as a multiple of your income. If you make $100,000 and your retirement accounts equal $200,000, you have saved two times.

Next find the row that is closest to your age.

The intersection of the savings column and the age row is the percentage of your gross income that you should be targeting to save.

		HOW MUCH YOU HAVE SAVED AS A MULTIPLE OF YOUR INCOME					
		0X	1X	2X	4X	6X	8X
CURRENT AGE	20	11%	5%	Funded	Funded	Funded	Funded
	25	15%	9%	3%	Funded	Funded	Funded
	30	21%	14%	8%	Funded	Funded	Funded
	35	28%	21%	15%	1%	Funded	Funded
	40	40%	32%	25%	10%	Funded	Funded
	45	58%	50%	42%	25%	9%	Funded
	50	90%	80%	70%	51%	31%	11%
	55	> 100%	> 100%	> 100%	> 100%	77%	51%
	60	> 100%	> 100%	> 100%	> 100%	> 100%	> 100%

Easy right? If your box said "Funded," you have technically saved enough to let your retirement assets ride until 65 and have enough to replace 90% of your current income. If this is you, I would still contribute to retirement accounts to keep up the habit and to prepare for unexpected changes in income or expenses. If your box said > 100%, you need to go back and play more financial offense. This may feel discouraging, but the math says that to replace 90% of your current income, you would need to save more than you make.

Keep in mind that this is very generalized. I have known high-income doctors, lawyers, and other professionals who made $400,000 to $800,000 per year, but only spent $100,000 in retirement. This table would not work for them.

For more complex scenarios, financial advisors have tools that simplify the process, but if you still want to DIY this, I will give you some math you can run. If the table was enough for you, Method 2 will be overkill and you can skip it.

To show you how serious I am about skipping Method 2, these arrows >>> will appear below this paragraph and then again at the beginning of the paragraph where you will pick back up. Use these arrows like all those Italian words at the top of sheet music that tell you to skip or play to a symbol. Alternatively, if you prefer movie-based examples, this is like the Star Gate portal will take you beyond Method 2. If you want the details in Method 2, you may brave the "fire swamp" …as you wish.

>>>

Method 2: The Nerd's Manual Math

You will not need any expensive planning software for this. You might want an excel file up for the formulas so you can recreate your output with several numbers.

1. **Consider Social Security:** Decide whether you want to factor in Social Security. If you do, look up your current benefit on SSA.gov. If you decide to assume Social Security will be around for you, then you will need to remember this number for step 3.

2. **Estimate Annual Expenses**: Most people do not have exact clarity on where their money is going. It is a project everyone should tackle and revisit, but we do not want that unpleasant task to get in the way of today's progress. There are two ways to estimate your expenses. Option A will get you moving even if you do not know your cash flow details well.

   a. The <u>Top-Down Estimate</u> is to use your current income as a guide. Start with your total current income (the top) and subtract expenses that will disappear when you retire. Primarily, the expenses that go away are your retirement plan contributions and the principal and interest portion of your mortgage payment if you pay off your home by retirement. You will still pay for healthcare and taxes (including property taxes) in retirement so do not subtract those.

b. The <u>Bottom-Up Estimate</u> is to list all your expenses manually and add them up. The biggest concern with this method is accounting for irregular expenses and lifestyle. For some people who do an excellent job tracking their finances, the bottom-up method works. For the other 99% of us, I have found the top-down method to be more relatable and frankly, more accurate.

3. **Decide on your withdrawal need & nest egg:** Your withdrawal need is the amount you expect to withdraw from your accounts in retirement. Let's say you wanted $150,000 of income and you are comfortable factoring in $40,000 of Social Security payments between you and your

spouse. This means your withdrawal need is $110,000. Multiply this number by 20 or 25. This will give you a target nest egg balance. Multiplying by 25 is more conservative as you will be targeting a larger number. In this case $110,000 X 25 is $2,750,000. You might wonder or even potentially worry about how to account for inflation on this withdrawal need. There is a straightforward way to account for that without having to build massive tables in excel or using fancy retirement projection tools. It is an inflation-adjusted return.

4. **Consider Inflation**: Use an inflation rate to adjust your future expenses. Inflation has been as high as 20% in the 1920s. On the other extreme side, we have seen deflation in the 1920s, the 1930s, 1940s, and 2009. To account for that variability, you are just going to use an average rate. A common rate to use is 3% per year. If you are more concerned about inflation, use 4% or 5%. Inflation is scary and most people become more concerned about it as they age. Keep in mind that during the last 50 years, inflation has been painful, but by the data, it has been tame compared to the 50 years prior to that.

5. **Calculate the inflation-adjusted return:** If you use an inflation-adjusted return, you do not have to adjust all the other factors for inflation. It makes life easier and the numbers more understandable. Here is how you do it:

   a. First you need to divide the return by inflation, but for the math to work out right, you need to use 1 + the return.

   b. For example, if you assume you will make 9% return, which is the same as 0.09, you need to do 1 + 0.09 which is 1.09. Follow the same rule for inflation. If we use 3% as our inflation amount, we will use 1.03 in the equation. It will look like this: (1+Return) / (1+Inflation) or (1.09/1.03) which is 1.05825.

   c. Next, subtract the 1 back out to leave you with 0.05825 which is the same as 5.825%. This is the inflation adjusted return for 9% growth and 3% inflation. Notice how you cannot just do 9% minus 3%? That would have been 6%. Compounding growth is funny like that.

6. **Run a Payment formula in Excel or Google Sheets:** The PMT or Payment formula tells you how much you need to save to hit the final goal. When you use an inflation-adjusted return, it assumes that you will save a little more each year to account for inflation. I like this method because it is more realistic than a 20-year-old trying to save the same amount as she could save at age 45 when her earnings are higher. The PMT formula will look like this: =PMT(.05825,25,-250000,2750000,0)

   a. 0.05825 is the inflation-adjusted return.

   b. 25 is the number of years until retirement.

   c. $250,000 is the amount this person has already saved. In a PMT formula, you must enter the starting amount as a negative number.

   d. $2,750,000 is the nest egg target to produce the $110,000 worth of withdrawals annually.

e. 0 or 1 is the method of choosing when you want to invest the payments, at the beginning of the year or the end. Either is fine with such a long time horizon.

The payment is $32,137. This means you would need to invest $32,137 per year to reach your goal. Next year you need to invest 3% more, which is $33,101.

Wow! If you made it through method 2, congratulations!

> >

If you skipped method 2, this is where you pick back up. We are going to use $30,000 as our target savings as we move into Task 2.

Task 2: Review Your Current Income and Tax Situation vs. Retirement Tax Situation

Understanding your current and future tax situations is vital for tax-efficient retirement planning. Knowing your marginal tax bracket now and estimating it for retirement helps you make informed decisions about which retirement accounts to use.

The 'Roth vs Traditional' decision is one of the first questions people ask. The debate is larger than I imagined. I first went on YouTube to explain it a year ago and the views on these videos are well over one million at the time of writing this. The comments are in the thousands, and I love the engagement. The first and most important part is to understand what I call "The Same Spendable" principle.

If you have $10,000 to invest and you pay the same tax rate now vs later, it produces the same spendable amount. An initial investment of $10,000 in a Traditional retirement account has no up-front tax cost. Let's say it doubles to $20,000. Then finally, you pay 25% tax to get it out. This leaves you with $15,000 spendable dollars. If you dedicated that same $10,000 to a Roth account, you must pay taxes up front subtracting the 25% from the start leaving you with $7,500 to invest. It doubles to $15,000 and you end up with the same spendable amount. Here is a quick visual that often helps people see both paths:

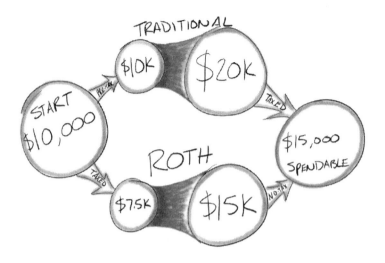

It will always work this way if the tax rate and the growth rates are the same. So, a difference in tax rates is important. Will your tax rate drop? If yes, do Traditional contributions. Will it rise? If yes, do Roth contributions. Will the government change tax rates? Do you feel like you would like to have control over your retirement tax picture by having retirement accounts in all tax structures? If yes, do a mixture of the two and invest in non-retirement accounts as well. These are all the questions you should ask yourself as you decide to allocate contributions to your retirement accounts. Do not fret over this complexity. At the end of this project, I am going to give you rules to make it easy.

Steps to Compare Tax Situations:

1. **Identify Current Marginal Tax Rate**: Look at your recent tax return to find the tax rate applied to your last dollar of income. You can do this by finding your taxable income on your 1040. It is usually near line 15 at the bottom of the first page. Now Google "marginal tax brackets." Lastly, find the bracket in which your taxable income falls. This is your marginal rate. Remember, this is the rate applied to the very last dollar of income you earned. It does not apply to all the income you earned.

2. **Estimate Retirement Income**: Predict your income sources in retirement, such as Social Security, pensions, and withdrawals from retirement accounts.

3. **Estimate Retirement Tax Bracket**: Based on your projected income, determine your tax bracket in retirement using the same process as step 1, but with your retirement income instead of your current income.

Task 3: Consider Whether You Will Try to Retire Before 59½ Years Old

Retiring before 59½ years old comes with unique challenges, primarily because of penalties on early withdrawals from retirement accounts.

Considerations for Early Retirement:

1. **Early Withdrawal Penalties**: Withdrawals from traditional retirement accounts before 59½ typically incur a 10% penalty plus taxes.
2. **Strategies to Avoid Penalties**: Investigate options like Roth IRA contributions (which you can withdraw penalty-free) and the Rule of 55 for 401(k) plans. There is also a rule called 72t or Separate Equal Periodic Payments (SEPP) that allows you to get access to your traditional IRAs before 59½ if you follow certain rules.
3. **Consider non-retirement accounts**: Building non-retirement wealth is Prosperity Project 6, however, if you plan to retire before 59½ , you should allocate some of your annual savings to non-IRA and non-401(k) accounts.

I had a client who believed he could not retire at age 56. He had enough money. He just thought there was no way around the retirement withdrawal rules at age 59½. Don't let tax rules determine important life decisions.

Task 4: Allocate Your Annual Savings to Various Tax Structures and Investments

Based on your goals and tax situation, allocate your savings across different retirement accounts to optimize tax benefits.

Allocation Strategies:

1. **Traditional 401(k) and Traditional IRA:** Contributions are tax-deferred, meaning you get a tax break now and pay taxes upon withdrawal in retirement.
2. **Roth 401(k) and Roth IRA:** You make contributions with after-tax dollars, but withdrawals in retirement are tax free.
3. **Brokerage Accounts:** If you hold investments long enough, you will pay the lower long-term

capital gains rates on investments in these accounts.

The Easy Rules Based on Your Tax Rate:

Once you have determined your savings goal, you need to save that money somewhere. The reality is that the amount you save is much more important than whether you save in a Traditional, Roth, or after-tax account. The first easy rule to remember is: Save the right amount. Without assets, you do not have a tax or investment problem, you have an everything problem.

Let's assume we are working with the example of saving $30,000 per year. Let's also assume you have a match on your 401(k). If so, you accomplish some of your $30,000 savings goal with the free money and the contributions you made to get your free money. Let's assume you are contributing $6,000 to get your match and the match is also $6,000 for a total of $12,000. This means you need to contribute another $18,000. I will call this $18,000 the "additional contributions."

Here are three rules of thumb that will help you know how to allocate your savings based on your tax rate. Remember, when I say "additional contributions" I mean your total savings goal minus the amounts you already saved in Project 2.

1. **If your current marginal tax rate is above 30%:** Contribute to your 401(k) with Traditional contributions. If you are eligible, do backdoor Roth contributions for the rest of your additional contributions. If you are not able to do backdoor Roth contributions, deposit the rest of your additional contributions to a non-retirement brokerage account. The reason backdoor Roth contributions might not work is because you have Traditional IRA money.

2. **If your current marginal tax rate is between 20% and 30%:** Max out your 401(k) with a 50/50 mix of Traditional and Roth contributions. If you are eligible, do standard Roth IRA contributions if not, do backdoor Roth IRA contributions for the rest of your additional contributions. If you are not able to do either Roth IRA contributions or backdoor Roth contributions, deposit the rest of your additional contributions to a non-retirement brokerage account.

3. **If your current marginal tax rate is below 20%:** Max out your 401(k) with Roth contributions. If you are eligible, do Roth contributions for the rest of your additional contributions. If you are

not able to do Roth or backdoor Roth contributions, deposit the rest of your additional contributions to a non-retirement brokerage account.

If this does not make sense, work through these examples with me.

Example 1: Susan

Here is an example of Susan, who has a high income and has a high savings goal:

Susan makes $250,000 per year. Her employer matches her income dollar for dollar on the first 6% of contributions. Her overall savings goal is $50,000 per year. Her marginal tax bracket is between 20% and 30%. Here are her steps:

1. Get free money by making a 6% contribution to her 401(k). She will make a $15,000 contribution based on 6% of $250,000. Her employer will also contribute $15,000. The match is commonly traditional tax status. She will do 3% Roth and 3% Traditional.

2. Her goal is $50,000 of savings and she will have saved $30,000 between her 6% contribution and the match.

3. The additional savings she still needs to make is $20,000. Let's assume the 401(k) max contribution limit was $23,000. She has used up $15,000 of that limit. She would be able to contribute another $8,000, which is about 3% of her income. She should contribute that to her 401(k) as Roth because her match is going in as Traditional. This will get her closer to a 50/50 split between the Roth and Traditional tax statuses. In the end, she will log into her 401(k) and put 6% Roth and 3% Traditional. The employer will put in another 6% Traditional. Could she just put all 9% in Roth or Traditional? Sure. Remember, the amount is more important than the tax status.

4. After her 15% savings to her 401(k) between her employer and her own contributions, Susan still needs to contribute $12,000 toward her retirement goal ($50,000 minus the 6% contribution of $15,000, the 6% match of $15,000, and the additional 3% Roth savings of $8,000). Susan should make a backdoor Roth contribution of $7,000 if eligible.

5. She will contribute $5,000 to a non-retirement brokerage account. She will do all $12,000 if she is not eligible for a backdoor Roth. This will finish off her $50,000 worth of contributions, get her free money, and diversify the tax structures.

Example 2: Jeff

Jeff has a more typical situation for a lot of 30-year-old savers. His income is not as high as Susan's.

Jeff makes $80,000 per year. His employer matches 4% if he contributes 5%. He has a goal of saving 14% of his pay because he used the easy chart and has about one time his income saved. Jeff's overall savings goal is $11,200. Jeff is married and has two kids. He also gives money to charities and has a mortgage. This all means he pays close to 0% in taxes.

1. Get free money by making a 5% contribution to his 401k. Jeff will contribute $4,000 of his own money to the 401(k). His match will be $3,200 because it is 4% of his pay for contributing 5%.
2. Jeff will do all his initial contributions as Roth given his low tax rate. His rate may be higher in the future when he earns more or loses the

dependent deductions for his kids after they move out.

3. His total savings from Project 2 (Get Free Money) will be $7,200. Jeff will contribute another $4,000 to his Roth 401(k) to achieve his annual savings goal of $11,200. He will be well below contributions limits.

4. Jeff could choose to contribute that last $4,000 to a Roth IRA instead of his Roth 401(k). The IRA will offer him better investment flexibility and options. The contribution to his 401(k) is easier to execute with automatic investments. Given his income and contribution goals, he will not bump up against IRS contribution limits in either option. Will he forget to make the IRA contribution if the money hits his bank account first? Will he spend it before saves any? Jeff should pick the option that will provide the easiest path to action. Even if his Roth 401(k) is more restricted in the investment options, it may still be better than the Roth IRA if the greater ease of the 401(k) is the only way Jeff contributes to either.

Task 5: Review Your Overall Savings Plan

Regularly reviewing your savings plan ensures that you are on track to meet your retirement goals and that your savings are tax efficient.

Review Steps:

1. **Savings Rate**: Ensure you are saving enough each year to reach your target retirement amount. You do this by checking the math in Task 1 of this Project 3.

2. **Tax Statuses**: Analyze the tax status of your accounts (tax-deferred, tax-free, taxable) and adjust contributions to balance your tax exposure. The next task will help you better understand why and how to do this.

Task 6: Consider Investing in All Three Tax Types

One more time, the amount saved is more important than the tax structure. However, it does not mean the tax structure does not matter. Diversifying your retirement savings across different tax statuses can provide flexibility and control over your taxes in retirement.

Investment Types:

1. **Tax-Deferred Accounts**: Traditional 401(k) and IRA. You invest money you haven't paid taxes on. You pay taxes on all the money you withdraw.

2. **Tax-Free Accounts**: Roth 401(k) and IRA. You invest after-tax money. You do not pay taxes on any of the money you withdraw.

3. **Taxable Accounts**: Non-retirement brokerage accounts. You invest after-tax money and pay taxes annually on income or gains from selling investments.

Benefits of Tax Diversification:

The main benefit is flexibility. Having multiple tax structures in your assets allows for better control over your tax situation in retirement.

If you start with the end in mind, it will be clearer. Let me describe a couple very similar to the one I met last week. This couple has $3,000,000, all sitting in their 401(k) in traditional tax status. In your early seventies, the IRS mandates withdrawals from Traditional tax status retirement accounts to force you to pay some taxes before you pass away. This age has been extended as people are living longer. The IRS requires a withdrawal of about 4% in the beginning, but that percentage ramps up as you age. In the beginning, your annual required distribution would be about $120,000. On top of that, this couple has other income from Social Security, a pension, taxable investments, and activities. They may be as high as $200,000 per year. None of this sounds terrible. In fact, it is quite good. They are avoiding the major penalties for high income on things like Medicare Part B premiums and they are in reasonable tax brackets. Their retirement tax status is better than their tax status was while working.

I am going to say it again because retirees are scared out of their minds over this, the tax situation described here is not bad! A strikingly similar version of this couple has sat in my office or over zoom meetings hundreds of times. They have felt more than a simple pang of fear; they envision a tax man forcefully knocking on their door ready to take all their savings. Financial advisors feed into this fear. It is easier to get you to act if you are agitated, but here is the truth: Today, a healthy Social Security income of $60,000 plus $120,000 of required distributions produces an 11.5% effective (average) Federal tax rate for a senior couple in the tax structure in the early to mid-2020s. They are not subject to Medicare Part B premium penalties. The limits for those are above $200,000 right now.

This senior couple is not the target of politicians who want to raise taxes. On paper, their income looks very upper-middle class even though their net worth is anything but middle class. In contrast, imagine a young 30-year-old couple, 5 years out of college, with two kids and both earning $100,000 after building momentum in their professional careers. They still have student debt, a large mortgage, and no assets. They have the same income as the senior couple, but a vastly different net worth. Those tax returns do not look vastly different. Like a zebra in a herd, your similar stripes do not completely protect you, but they make you hard to target.

Could it be better for this senior couple? Imagine instead that the couple diversified their $3,000,000 across different tax structures. What if $500,000 was Traditional, $1,250,000 was Roth, and $1,250,000 was non-retirement brokerage assts or investment real estate? They could have the same spendable amount each year in retirement (if not more) and pay much less in taxes. In addition to a lower income from required distributions from retirement accounts, a couple at this level gets a tax break on their Social Security income. Their required withdrawal would be about $20,000, they have $60,000 of Social Security, and $35,000 of dividends and interest if managed carefully. This means that not all their Social Security income is taxable. Specifically, 68% would be taxable. Their effective (average) tax rate would be 6.2%.

So why not only contribute to Roth and brokerage accounts if the tax situation can be so favorable in retirement? It is not so simple; you must first ask: What did it cost you to get there? It is not worth paying a 30% tax on your income while working to avoid a 12% tax in retirement. If this concept is still not hitting home, find my Roth vs Traditional YouTube videos or podcast episodes. The "Same Spendable" principle I cover will help.

Back to the senior couple, a diversified tax structure creates flexibility for large expenses. What if they want to buy a car? If all their money is in the traditional tax status, this may force them over tax lines that are painful. If they have Roth or non-retirement assets, they may be able to draw from those accounts and avoid certain penalties or lines.

Prosperity Project 3 Wrap Up

By following these six tasks, you can optimize your retirement tax benefits and plans, setting yourself up for a financially secure and comfortable retirement. The key is to start planning now, stay informed, and adjust your strategies as your circumstances change. With detailed instructions and actionable advice, this chapter empowers you to take control of your retirement planning with confidence.

If you made it through Project 3, you are doing better than most Americans at organizing your wealth and achieving financial goals. Be proud and be excited. Reward yourself somehow. With each project that you pass, you can afford to slow down and think about your money differently. You were in emergency mode in Project 1. You completed Project 2 with urgency, but with less fear. Project 3 is much more strategic and done with a clear mind and patience. The money issues that you will address in Project 4 are more about aligning your values and wealth and less about preventing disasters or putting out fires. There might be tough questions to answer. Good thing you have earned the time to answer them now. Congratulations!

Prosperity Project 3 Checklist

- ☐ Task 1: Determine How Much Money You Need to Save to Hit Your Retirement Goal
  - ○ Method 1: The Easy Table.
  - ○ Method 2: The Nerd's Manual Math
- ☐ Task 2: Review Your Current Income and Tax Situation vs. Retirement Tax Situation
- ☐ Task 3: Consider Whether You Will Try to Retire Before 59½ Years Old
- ☐ Task 4: Allocate Your Annual Savings to Various Tax Structures and Investments
- ☐ Task 5: Review Your Overall Savings Plan
- ☐ Task 6: Consider Investing in All Three Tax Types

Next, we will talk about the people in your life and who should oversee your money, health, and assets if you are unable.

Zaccary Call

Prosperity Project 4: Decide Who Is in Charge

The process of documenting who will oversee your money, children, assets, and healthcare decisions is called "Estate Planning". There are two primary tasks in this project.

1. Foundational estate planning
2. Beneficiaries and ownership instructions.

Ideally, you would progress through these two tasks in order which means you would create your foundational estate plan and then name beneficiaries on your assets, but realistically it almost never happens that way. Most people do not put a foundational estate plan in place

Zaccary Call

until they have assets to protect or instructions to document. You will cross the decision threshold of beneficiary designations before you create a trust.

Most people misunderstand how early they should create a foundational estate plan. If you have a home, you almost always need a trust. If you have children, you need a will. If you want to prepare for the possibility of major health concerns, you need a power of attorney document and a healthcare directive. Those are early indicators that it is time for you to dial in your foundational estate planning. You can find professionals and solutions that are affordable. If you are having a challenging time understanding the options for estate planning professionals, find me on LinkedIn, YouTube, or other social media and I can introduce you to available resources.

These tasks are listed as sequential (1 and 2 vs A and B). However, you have likely already made some beneficiary decisions before reaching Task 2. If so, use Task 2 as an opportunity to review all listed beneficiaries on your accounts and assets.

Task 1: Foundational Estate Planning

If you pass away, the glue that holds families together could easily soften. Financial advisors and estate planners witness it often. Even if you believe your children will work together well, their spouses might not. Unfortunately, it is common for an estate settling process to drive a wedge so deep between your children that they never speak again. That is an extreme example, but some resentment and hurt feelings are not uncommon. Do your family a favor by organizing your wishes before you leave.

A foundational estate plan covers the following elements:

- Trust
- Will (with Guardianship instructions for minors if applicable)
- Power of Attorney
- Healthcare Directives

Trust – For death and disability

Your trust is a set of instructions and rules for your financial assets. It will survive beyond your lifespan. It instructs the trustee to act in your place. The basic trust is a revocable trust. This means you can revoke or change the trust until you pass away. At death, the trust becomes irrevocable. The trust will own your assets. Your trustee will distribute assets at the right time to the right people. Without a trust, your primary residence will often go through probate which is a costly, time-consuming, and annoying legal process in which a judge follows many steps to determine who is the rightful owner of your assets. A simple revocable trust can avoid all that confusion.

Will – For death

A will is a set of instructions for a judge in probate. Even if you have a trust, most people should also have a will. The will can help your other assets spill into the trust even if you have not officially turned over ownership of those assets to the trust during your lifetime. For example, most people do not change the title of their vehicles to their trust. Nor can you name a direct beneficiary of your car with the local motor vehicle department. How does the court handle that? The will pours that asset into the trust. However, I would not count on this as a failsafe for larger and more important assets. You should not leave those up to chance.

A will also allows you to make specific requests that certain individuals receive important items. This is common for sentimental items like a wedding ring or other family keepsakes.

Most importantly, if you have minor children, you should include instructions in your will for guardianship of your children until they are adults. Do not leave this decision to a judge. You may have documented guardianship instructions as part of solving for the big "what ifs" in Project 1. However, many people do not get to it that early. Either way, it is time to have the most difficult discussion of all. This is where you find out just how your spouse really feels about your siblings. As you discuss who should rear your children, you might be surprised at just how crazy your partner thinks your siblings are.

Nothing quite compares to the difficulty of trusting another adult with your children forever. It can be easy to put these decisions off. However, relationships sour faster over guardianship rights than over assets. This makes sense given the irreplaceable nature of your children vs the ability to earn another dollar.

You should talk to the designated individuals about this responsibility to see if they would feel honored and willing to help, or if they would like to pass.

Power of Attorney – For disability or convenience

A Power of Attorney document (POA) is an important authorization for someone to act on your behalf during your lifetime. This can be helpful in the case of disability, incapacity, or pure convenience. Spouses often designate each other as their POA to authorize each other with financial institutions. If you execute this document prior to an event of incapacity, especially mental incapacity, it is much easier to obtain. Imagine if your child must prove to a financial institution that you cannot mentally handle your financial affairs. Your family would need to engage both a doctor and an attorney at the same time to prove the necessity of a POA and then execute the document. This could be against your wishes. The result is that most people do not engage a doctor to avoid an uncomfortably intrusive situation. The result is the owner's finances suffer.

A friend of mine did not button up these instructions for both his power of attorney and trust documents. He experienced diminished capacity and within a year was not able to understand his assets, financial plan, or investments. The family was able to access one account due to proper documentation of authorization, however, the account was the traditional IRA. It was the least tax efficient for withdrawals. Even though there were Roth IRAs and brokerage accounts, they did not want to hurt his feelings by introducing a third party to assess his mental state. The family paid many thousands of dollars away in taxes above what was necessary, and they waited until he passed. The whole experience was heartbreaking for the family in so many ways. I understand why they made the decisions they made. Rightfully, the tax burden was the least of their concerns.

At death, a POA is no longer valid. The will and trust will guide those in charge to reregister the wealth to the new owners.

Trusts have their own succession plan for trustees. A POA is commonly rejected by financial institutions for trust assets. Also, you don't put your IRA in the name of a trust while living. This is why you need both a trust and power of attorney documents.

Healthcare Directive – For disability and clarity

There are important instructions to document in order to guide your loved ones around how to make important healthcare decisions for you if you cannot communicate your wishes. These can be heart-wrenching decisions to make for someone else. It can alleviate a major burden on your loved ones if you have instructions in place. The alternative is to put your loved ones in a forever state of doubt about whether they made the right choices for you.

You will know that you have been successful at Task 1 of Foundational Estate Planning if you have all these documents in a safe place and you have executed them with signatures. When you get to this point, you are not done! Let's keep moving into Task 2.

Task 2: Create your Net Worth Statement

This is a simple task that is often overlooked. You need a method for organizing everything you own and debts you owe. In accounting, this is called a "balance sheet."

In financial planning, this is called a "Net Worth Statement." Most financial planners and financial experts will tell you this should have been Project 1. However, people find net worth calculations to be overwhelming that early in the planning process. Also, I want you to see progress first. Now that you have momentum and some success behind you, net worth statements are a more positive and productive experience.

Why Build a Net Worth Statement?

1. Make sure you don't forget assets. This is precisely why we are working on it right now. We are about to ensure your estate plan is properly applied to your wealth. It would be a shame to forget an asset and force your heirs into a frustrating legal process after your passing.

2. Allow your beneficiaries to have one document they can use as a checklist for settling your estate.

3. Allow you to see your overall exposure to different investments or asset types.

4. Mark your progress on a periodic basis so you can see how your wealth is changing over time. Many of us feel behind, nervous,

or even discouraged at the lack of growth in our assets. We all wonder if we are doing okay. When you revisit the old net worth statements, you will be surprised at the positive progress.

Now that you understand *why* to build a net worth statement, you may be wondering *how* to build one. A financial advisor can help; however, the primary point of this book was to provide anyone—a DIYer or delegator—the tools to be financially successful. By Googling, "Personal Balance Sheet Tool" or "Personal Balance Sheet Excel" you will find more options than you need. I would always include the word "personal" in your search. Otherwise, you will get options that are built for large companies with things like "Shareholders' Equity" which doesn't apply to your personal financial household.

These tools will all be built around a simple formula:

Assets minus Liabilities equals Net Worth.

That's it.

List Your Assets:

Make a list of all the things you own. Include the full value of the asset. For example, a house worth $700,000 with a $250,000 mortgage gets listed as $700,000 in the asset column.

I like to group my assets up into different categories. Here is my list so you can have some structure if you choose to build your own balance sheet.

- Retirement: List each Roth, IRA, 401(k), and brokerage account.
- Cash: List each bank account.
- Real Estate: List each piece of real estate property you own. For example, your primary residence, other raw land, or rental properties.
- General Investment: List other funds or investments that don't fit well within Retirement, Cash, or Real Estate.
- Business Ownership: List the value of your business if you are self-employed. List the value of any other small businesses you may own.
- Personal Items: List things like cars, jewelry, and valuable personal items. At one point, my mountain bike was the next most valuable item I owned after our cars and my wife's wedding ring,

so I listed it. The bike wasn't top of the line. For context, at this time we owned three cars all worth a combined value of $11,000. You may list anything worth more than a few thousand dollars. You might decide to only list items worth more than $25,000 depending on your willingness to get into detail and the value of your overall net worth.

- Miscellaneous: Lastly, I list my kids' college savings funds and donor advised funds. I do not include the balance of either of those in my net worth calculation, but I like to have them on the same page.

List Your Debts:

Make a list of all the debts you owe. Include the name of the debt ("Ford Car Loan"), who you owe it to ("ABC Credit Union"), and outstanding balance of the debt ("$22,000").

I wouldn't break the debt into various categories like we did for your assets. Hopefully there aren't that many categories or actual debts to keep track of. Just put them all in a list.

Calculate Your Net Worth:

Sum up your assets. Sum up your debts. Subtract debts from your assets. This is your net worth. Do not analyze yourself or give yourself a grade. Your only goal in this step is to organize it and create a starting point. You can analyze yourself in six to twelve months when you revisit this sheet and mark progress. In the beginning, progress is the goal, not a specific number. As you see progress and get closer to retirement, you should start benchmarking your different categories to the goal for that category. For example, your retirement goal vs retirement assets. Another example might be a debt reduction goal. You might determine you want to pay off your car by a certain date. You could track your progress to that goal with your net worth statement.

Task 3: Beneficiaries & Ownership Instructions

When you finish signing and printing your estate plan, you will be so excited. It is hard to contemplate your own demise. It is mentally taxing to make such impactful and emotional decisions. You will be holding your signed documents. The documents might be bound together in some fashion, and you may feel like you are done. As finished as the plan may seem to you, it is like having signed a car rental agreement and the rental company handing you the keys. You have the right to drive a car, but you are not in the vehicle yet nor have you gotten to your destination.

Once your foundational estate plan is in place, it is time to review all your assets and accounts specifically to ensure you have assigned the right transfer instructions. It is not enough to list an asset in the trust documents. The financial institution must know about it as well. If the financial institution has different beneficiary instructions than your trust, the instructions the institution has on their form signed by the deceased owner will overpower anything you write in your trust.

Let's repeat that. Your IRA provider doesn't care what your trust says. They will only reference the named beneficiaries on their own system with the owner's signature.

There are four ways to ensure that you have proper instructions in place:

1. Assign beneficiary designations.
2. Change ownership to the trust now.

3. Use the trust as the beneficiary.
4. Create a separate document.

It is important to understand that state laws vary and that what follows are general guidelines and not specific legal rules/interpretations.

Assign Beneficiary Designations

A beneficiary will be able to inherit your account and bypass the probate process. The beneficiary will provide a copy of your death certificate and some sort of identification proving they are the beneficiary. At that point, the financial institution will help them "reregister" the assets into their own name. Normally, the beneficiary will open an account in their own name and then the financial institution will transfer the assets from your account to the newly established one in their name. Beneficiary designations are often the simplest and cleanest way of passing on assets to someone else.

Change Ownership to the Trust Now

For some assets and accounts you can make your trust the owner instead of you. If it is a revocable trust, you have not completed any actual transfer of ownership yet, so you are not "selling" the asset to a trust. This means there is no tax consequence of reregistering the asset to the trust. This is appropriate for real estate, bank accounts, non-retirement brokerage accounts. If you cannot name a beneficiary, changing ownership to the trust is important. Unfortunately, it is often a forgotten step. Even if you can name beneficiaries, there are reasons some people use a trust instead of standard beneficiary designations.

A friend of mine and her husband thought their home was properly registered. They were joint owners with a status called "tenants in common." The husband passed. The wife had to put his portion of the home through probate. She had to go through probate to keep her own home. Joint ownership with rights of survivorship could have avoided probate, however, a trust would have easily solved this as well.

Use the Trust as the Beneficiary

You cannot move a retirement account out of your own name without withdrawing it all and paying taxes. One way to have your trust wishes executed on your retirement accounts is by naming your trust as the beneficiary. This may have some tax consequences for your beneficiaries that force them to withdraw the funds at a faster rate after your passing. We will not cover all the rules for trusts as IRA beneficiaries in this book. However, the gist is that a trust as a beneficiary may force the beneficiaries to withdraw the funds sooner causing more taxes to be paid. The tax rates can be higher. Also, direct beneficiary inherited IRA accounts are often simpler to administer requiring less paperwork and red tape.

There is a straightforward way to make this decision. Ask yourself two questions: 1. Do I worry about my beneficiary inheriting this much money all at once? 2. Does my trust have restrictions that can help protect this beneficiary from themself? If the answer is yes to both, you should name your trust as the beneficiary of your retirement accounts. If the answer is yes to #1 and no to #2, it is time to build language into your trust to protect your beneficiary. If the answer is no to #1 and yes to #2, it is time to remove some restrictive language in your trust. Generally, directly-named beneficiary designations make it much easier on your heirs and for this reason, many account owners prefer direct designations to individuals.

Here is a less common case in which the trust was needed as the IRA beneficiary. I helped manage the assets of a trust for the benefit of a surviving daughter of a hard-working woman. The daughter was in her 30's, but unfortunately, she struggled with addiction. The mother knew of her daughter's struggles before she passed and built rules into her trust requiring a series of clean drug tests to access funds from the trust. The mother put her brother on as the trustee (the daughter's uncle). The daughter had opportunities every 5 years to prove her sobriety, but unfortunately, she never passed. The assets were eventually given to another purpose that was listed as plan B in the trust. Whether you agree with the mother's decisions is not the lesson. The important thing to understand is that if the daughter had been listed directly as a beneficiary, she would have had access to the entire IRA immediately.

Create a Separate Document

I have an LLC. It is a simple one, but it has some assets built up inside it. Right now, I am the only member of the LLC. This makes it easy to operate. There are no employees other than me. How would the bank know who oversees the LLC checking account and other assets if I passed away? They will not just take my wife's word for it. What if I had a business partner that was not my spouse? Who has the first rights to the assets? LLCs do not have beneficiary designations. They normally have a buy-sell agreement. Insurance agents like to talk about buy-sell agreements as if they are insurance policies, but the agreement is a document outlining the rights, rules, and timing of the business ownership if death or other events happen. It can be helpful to use life insurance to fund the buy-sell agreement, but do not confuse the insurance with the agreement.

A buy-sell agreement does not make any sense if the assets belong to my wife. She just needs to inherit any assets owned by the LLC. My estate planner helped me draft an official document in which we identify my wife as the successor member of the LLC upon my passing. With this document and my death certificate, she should be able to remove me and add herself as a signer on all the accounts.

Prosperity Project 4 Wrap Up

Once you are safe from financial ruin and you are optimizing your retirement options, it is time to ensure you protect your family relationships from money difficulties. That is what Project 4 is all about. Put the right people in charge. Put the right decisions down on paper. Create clarity and show your love with a foundational estate plan.

Prosperity Project 4 Checklist

- ☐ Task 1: Foundational Estate Planning
    - o Trust – For death and disability
    - o Will – For death
    - o Power of Attorney – For disability or convenience
    - o Healthcare Directive – For disability and clarity
- ☐ Task 2: Create your Net Worth Statement
    - o Why Build a Net Worth Statement?
    - o List Your Assets
    - o List Your Debts
    - o Calculate Your Net Worth
- ☐ Task 3: Beneficiaries & Ownership Instructions
    - o Assign Beneficiary Designations
    - o Change Ownership to The Trust Now
    - o Use the Trust as the Beneficiary
    - o Create a Separate Document

Zaccary Call

Prosperity Project 5: Reduce Unwanted Debt

Before we move on to Projects 5, 6, and 7, I have a confession. I wouldn't be heartbroken if you stopped reading here. Think about it. If you completed Projects 1 through 4, your financial picture looks like this:

- Strong emergency fund
- Life, disability, and liability insurance
- Foundational Estate Plan: Will, trust, POA, healthcare directive, guardianship
- No high interest debt
- Getting free money
- Saving enough for retirement
- Saving into multiple account types

- On track for normal retirement

This is so much better than most Americans.

However, if you continue reading, you will learn some pro tips in the next three projects. For those of you moving on, let's talk about the rest of debt...not the high-interest kind.

By this point in your financial journey, you should have already tackled the most pressing and costly financial obligations, such as high-interest debt. What remains are debts that are typically lower interest and tied to essential or reasonable assets like your home and car. This chapter will guide you through the strategic management of these remaining debts and help you make informed decisions about when and how to pay them down or leverage them to further build your wealth.

Task 1: Managing Reasonable Debt

Given that you have eliminated high-interest debt, your remaining debts should be at lower interest rates. This debt should be strategic or for necessary purposes like a reasonable home and reasonable cars. It is essential to recognize that not all debt is bad. If your car and home are reasonable and the interest rates on your debt are low, you are okay to keep this debt while you move on to building greater wealth instead of focusing solely on paying it down with your next dollars.

Types of "Reasonable" Debt

- **Reasonable Home:** Ensure your mortgage is affordable, and the home suits your needs without stretching your budget. Your car, your home, and taxes are likely to be your biggest expenses. You have little control over the tax code. You have control over your cars and home. I witnessed a couple who argued about money, both felt poor, both struggled to enjoy their fifties because they owned two large homes and were unwilling to downsize either. After the real estate expenses, they lived on a very modest budget. It was strange to feel sorry for someone with such a large net worth, but they were house rich and cashflow poor. It is your decision, but sometimes it is a tough one. Not even your advisor wants to say it aloud, but you might need to move.

- **Reasonable Car:** Your vehicle should be dependable and affordable, not an item that strains your finances. Most people overbuy cars. In some cultures, the car you drive defines your status. Be careful. Again, your car and your home will dictate your disposable cashflow. If you need to, quantify it. For example, what would you do with $2,400 each year? You can have that if you reduce your car expense by $200 per month.

- **Low-Interest Rates:** Low-interest debt in moderation rarely impacts your long-term financial goals.

Task 2: Comparing Investment Returns with Debt Interest Rates

Before deciding whether to pay down your remaining debt or invest, it is crucial to compare your expected investment rate of return against your debt interest rate. Since paying down debt has a guaranteed return (reducing the interest owed), while investing has a potential but not guaranteed return, you need to adjust your comparison.

Risk Adjusted Return Rule of Thumb:

- Multiply your debt interest rate by 1.25 to 1.5.
- The expected investment rate of return needs to be greater than 1.25-1.5 times your debt interest rate.

Example:

- If your debt interest rate is 4%, multiply it by 1.25 to 1.5, resulting in 5% to 6%.
- Your expected investment return should be greater than 5% to 6% to justify investing instead of paying down debt.

Why the Adjustment?

- Debt repayment offers a guaranteed benefit—every dollar paid towards debt reduces your interest owed.
- Investments carry risk and do not guarantee a return, hence there is the need for a higher expected rate to compensate for this uncertainty. The more conservative you feel about money decisions, the bigger your

adjustment factor should be. If you are nervous about investing, increase the factor to 2 or 3.

Task 3: Debt Avalanche vs. Debt Snowball

For those who choose to pay down reasonable debt, revisiting the Debt Avalanche and Debt Snowball methods can be beneficial.

Debt Avalanche Method:

- Focuses on paying off debts with the highest interest rates first, saving you more money overall.
- Pay minimum payments on all debts, then apply any extra money to the highest interest debt.

Debt Snowball Method:

- Focuses on paying off the smallest debts first, giving you quick wins and building momentum
- Pay minimum payments on all debts, then apply any extra money to the smallest debt

Choosing the Right Method:

- Debt Avalanche: Ideal if long-term saving motivates you and have the discipline to stick with it
- Debt Snowball: Ideal if you need quick wins and psychological boosts to stay motivated

Task 4: Debt as a Wealth-Building Tool

Remember that debt can be a tool to enhance wealth if used properly. For instance, small businesses often require capital to grow, whether to hire more staff or open additional locations. Strategic use of debt in such cases can be the primary factor preventing growth and achieving greater financial success.

When to purposefully incur debt for wealth building:

- Business Growth: Using debt to invest in business expansion can lead to increased revenue and profits.

119

- Personal Preference: At this stage, deciding to pay down reasonable debt is a personal preference rather than a commandment. Evaluate your comfort level and financial goals to make the best decision for your situation.

Prosperity Project 5 Wrap Up

Revisit your car loans and mortgages. Consider your interest rate and do not forget the difference between risk-adjusted rates. Use debt as a tool only if prudent and your risk tolerance allows for it. Plenty of people get rich without using debt to get there. Celebrate that you are so good at money decisions!

Prosperity Project 5 Checklist

- ☐ Task 1: Managing Reasonable Debt
- ☐ Task 2: Comparing Investment Returns with Debt Interest Rates
- ☐ Task 3: Debt Avalanche vs. Debt Snowball

Your next project is where the wealthy stand out. They have succeeded at Project 6 "Build Non-Retirement Wealth.

Prosperity Project 6: Build Non-Retirement Wealth

This section will delve into the importance and benefits of creating wealth outside of retirement accounts like IRAs and 401(k)s. You can achieve a solid retirement plan if you stop after Project 5. However, building non-retirement wealth offers additional flexibility, tax advantages, and opportunities for growth that can significantly enhance your financial well-being. Even if you decide Projects 1 through 5 were enough, it is worth understanding the tax structure the wealthy use to build and preserve their assets.

Task 1: Understand Non-Retirement Wealth

Non-retirement wealth refers to assets and investments outside of retirement-specific accounts. These can include real estate, small businesses, and standard brokerage accounts. The wealthiest individuals often have substantial holdings in these types of assets, providing them with greater financial freedom and more options for managing their finances.

Some people will need to utilize non-retirement brokerage accounts and other non-retirement investment options to reach their annual savings goal from Project 3. This happens because their annual contribution goal is more than the IRS allows for contributions to retirement accounts.

Some people do not like the IRS withdrawal rules and prefer greater flexibility. In Project 3, they will need to make all their investments or contributions to non-retirement accounts or assets.

Task 2: Understand the Benefits of Investing Outside of IRAs and 401(k)s

Flexibility:

- **Access to Funds:** Unlike retirement accounts, you can access most non-retirement investments at any time without penalties. This means you can use these funds for major life events, emergencies, or investment opportunities as they arise.
- **No Mandatory Distributions:** Retirement accounts like IRAs and 401(k)s require you to start taking distributions at a certain age, but non-retirement accounts do not have such requirements, allowing you to manage your withdrawals according to your needs.

Tax Management:

- **Long-Term Capital Gains Rates:** Investments held for more than a year in a standard brokerage account are eligible for long-term capital gains tax rates, which are generally lower than ordinary income tax rates. This can result in significant tax savings over time.

- **Tax-Loss Harvesting**: Non-retirement accounts offer opportunities for tax-loss harvesting, where you can sell investments at a loss to offset gains and reduce your taxable income.

Diversification:

- **Broader Investment Choices**: Non-retirement accounts allow you to invest in a wider range of assets, including individual stocks, bonds, mutual funds, ETFs, real estate, and small businesses. This diversification can reduce risk and enhance potential returns.
- **Different Tax Treatments**: By having both retirement and non-retirement investments, you can take advantage of different tax treatments to optimize your overall tax situation.

Task 3: Explore Non-Retirement Investment Options

Standard Brokerage Accounts:

- **Overview**: These accounts allow you to buy and sell a variety of securities, such as stocks, bonds, and mutual funds. They are easy to set up and provide complete control over your investment decisions.
- **Benefits**: Flexibility in investment choices, potential for long-term capital gains tax rates, and the ability to withdraw funds without penalties.

Real Estate:

- **Overview**: Investing in real estate can include purchasing rental properties, commercial properties, or land. Real estate can provide a steady income stream and potential for appreciation.
- **Benefits**: Tangible assets with intrinsic value, potential for rental income, tax deductions

related to property expenses, and long-term appreciation. Real estate is special because of two things: 1. Depreciation and 2. Leverage. The government lets you reduce the amount of income you must report because the tax code says eventually that house will need to be fixed or torn down. Rather than wait until the day you tear down the house to claim the loss on your taxes, the government lets you take a partial loss each year. That is depreciation. Leverage is the idea of only owning a portion of an asset but getting the price increase of the entire asset. That goes both ways. Leverage is what brought many families to bankruptcy and short sales in the 2008 real estate crisis, but it has made many more people wealthy over decades.

Small Businesses:

- **Overview**: Starting or investing in a small business can be a significant wealth-building strategy. This can include owning a business outright or being a silent partner.
- **Benefits**: Potential for high returns, control over business decisions, and tax advantages related to business expenses and income.

Task 4: Implement a Non-Retirement Wealth Strategy

1. **Set Clear Goals:**

    ○ Determine what you want to achieve with your non-retirement investments. Are you looking for additional income, capital appreciation, or a safety net for emergencies?

2. **Diversify Your Investments:**

    ○ Spread your investments across different asset classes to minimize risk and maximize potential returns. Consider a mix of real estate, small businesses, and standard brokerage accounts.

3. **Monitor and Adjust:**

    ○ Regularly review your investment portfolio to ensure it aligns with your goals and risk tolerance. Adjust as needed based on market conditions and your financial situation.

4. **Consult with a Financial Advisor:**

   ○ Hiring a financial advisor can help you develop a comprehensive non-retirement wealth strategy tailored to your individual needs and goals.

   ○ Keep in mind that some financial advisors don't understand or specialize in non-retirement investments. Interview your advisor well.

Build Non-Retirement Wealth Your Way

The goal is not to build every type of non-retirement asset. The goal is to build non-retirement assets in your way. Some people hate the idea of managing properties and being a landlord. Others do not want the responsibility of having customers in a small business. You might be unwilling or unable to lock up your money in private investment funds with redemption restrictions.

You might not want to invest in public markets. People find many creative ways to make money outside of retirement accounts.

It is important to note that self-directed retirement accounts allow an investor to buy real estate or other non-traditional investments within an IRA wrapper, but that is less common and comes with some additional complexity vs investing in those same things with non-retirement money.

Doctors, lawyers, dentists, business managers and many other professionals have the potential to build wealth. However, if you are asking who creates the most wealth, it is business owners. Even those who own a small business often sell for several million dollars near retirement if they prepare well. In the most expensive neighborhoods I know, the doctors and lawyers are the least wealthy.

As you think about non-retirement investing in your own way, let me give you a couple questions to ask yourself which will narrow down your potential opportunities to pursue.

- Do you understand the investment opportunity better than most?
- Do you have access to an investment opportunity other people do not?
- Is researching this investment opportunity fun for you?
- Do you see the risks and are still willing to assume them because you understand the risks better?
- Is there complexity in the opportunity that does not seem complex to you?

These are questions that help you identify an opportunity.

An architect and a photographer are friends of my wife and me. We met as newlyweds living near each other while finishing college. After 5-8 years into their respective careers, they spotted an opportunity. The photographer could not find well-designed indoor photoshoot spaces. Instead of complaining about the lack of options, they created a business that offers beautifully designed and staged locations for other photographers to rent. Did they have an advantage? Absolutely. They understood the opportunity better. The architect could design, build, and execute the construction process. The photographer understood the lighting and selected stores with windows in the right locations. They found joy in researching the locations and capturing light in diverse ways. These complexities that would have overwhelmed me at the time seemed simple to them.

I am more comfortable with stock analysis and selection. I keep track of 50 individual stocks and their metrics on the side for fun. These friends are less comfortable with the idea of analyzing a stock's intrinsic value.

To get personal with you, my primary non-retirement wealth strategies are:

1. We build equity in our wealth management business in which I am a partner.
2. We deposit monthly to a non-retirement brokerage account and buy growth investments.
3. Every several years, we get involved in investment real estate. The initial investments are larger with real estate so you may need to do them less frequently so you can save up. Avoid over concentrating in one type of investment due to minimums.

4. We contribute to private equity investment funds with some money each year

They are in this order for a reason. The option I think will have the highest percentage return is my partnership equity in our wealth management business. The options with the highest probability of a reasonable and steady return over 5-10 years are the non-retirement brokerage accounts and real estate. I feel least confident in private equity solutions. I believe they will be successful, and I invest in them for diversification. I have friends who make most all their money as private equity fund managers. However, it comes back to advantages and personal interest. These friends have the advantage of understanding the risks, opportunities, and complexities of private investment options because they work in that industry.

Prosperity Project 6 Wrap Up

Building non-retirement wealth is a crucial component of a high-net-worth comprehensive financial plan. By investing outside of traditional retirement accounts, you gain greater flexibility, tax advantages, and opportunities for growth.

Prosperity Project 6 Checklist

- ☐ Task 1: Understand Non-Retirement Wealth
- ☐ Task 2: Understand the Benefits of Investing Outside of IRAs and 401(k)s
    - ○ Flexibility
    - ○ Tax Management
    - ○ Diversification
- ☐ Task 3: Explore Non-Retirement Investment Options
    - ○ Standard Brokerage Accounts
    - ○ Real Estate
    - ○ Small Businesses
- ☐ Task 4: Implement a Non-Retirement Wealth Strategy

Project 7 is where investing is more of a game. If you build enough wealth and you have enough income, you will not worry as much about taking risks.

Zaccary Call

Prosperity Project 7: Swing for the Fences

Welcome to the last prosperity project in your financial journey: "Swing for the Fences". By reaching this point, you have diligently worked through the foundational projects that form the bedrock of your financial stability. You have plugged the holes in your boat, harnessed the power of free money, optimized your retirement tax benefits and plans, reduced unwanted debt, and built non-retirement wealth. Now, you have earned the right to consider taking on additional investment risks with the potential for significant rewards.

In this chapter, we will explore high-risk, high-reward investment options. Remember, these strategies are entirely optional. You do not need to swing for the fences to achieve financial security and wealth. However, if you are comfortable with the possibility of higher volatility and potential losses, these opportunities might help you significantly grow your wealth over the next 2-4 years.

There is not a massive difference between Project 6 and Project 7. The key difference is risk and return. If an investment has a high probability of success with modest risk, it is a Project 6 non-retirement wealth builder. If an investment could go to zero or triple within a few years, it is more of a "Swing for the Fences."

Let me give you examples of some good and bad luck I have had in the last 5 years from swinging for the fences.

First, the bad: I had some friends experience some success with fast-casual restaurants coming out of COVID. I allocated money to a pool with the purpose of launching 10 stores within a single restaurant brand. The business planned to set up ten different stores within this brand. Last I heard, they made it to 4 or 5 stores all of which were operating at a loss. At this moment, I have not written off the loss on my tax returns, but I am not holding my breath. Losing this investment amount would not impact my family's overall finances, but it was enough to be very painful. This is the point of Project 7. You should size your bet in a way that it will not destroy any of the work you have done in Projects 1 through 6.

Second, the good luck: I learned to speak Spanish while living in Argentina in my early 20's for two years. I love the language, and I love Latin culture. If Argentina were closer, I would visit often. Visiting Mexico has been a more accessible way for me to practice Spanish and go on vacations with my family. While near Los Cabos, a friend of mine stumbled upon an area with very underdeveloped beachfront properties. In a later trip, my wife and I decided to check out the lots. It was so rural; I was concerned my little crossover SUV rental car would get stuck in the deep sand on the dusty and unmaintained pathways. Based on the route, I thought my friend had lost his mind until I saw the lots and homes. The Sea of Cortez was calm, and the sunset was beautiful. I wanted to stand and freeze time. I still cannot believe we went through with purchasing a lot. To purchase a lot, we had to hire an accountant in Mexico and provide a power of attorney to him to sign important legal contracts on our behalf. We had to navigate legal contracts, Mexican corporations, Mexican bank accounts, and negotiations in another country. At times, we only discussed those items in Spanish. While owning the lot, the Four Seasons hotel chain expanded in the area. The Aman hotel chain announced its plans to build a large luxury hotel. We visited the lot a few times over the next several years and determined we were unlikely to have the time and money to build a short-term rental home on the property like we had originally planned. Given the change in our family dynamics and time, we chose to sell the lot. The nearby hotel developments and other new construction pushed the price up and we sold it for a fair amount more than our purchase price. What was our advantage?... a lot of luck. Beyond the luck, we had a greater comfortability than most would with the risks, opportunity, and complexity of buying, owning, and selling land overseas.

Between the good and bad luck of these two investments we are net positive. We mostly laugh at the loss and made good friends in both investments. Overall, it was a success. However, if you experienced heavy stress and heartache, or you do not think you can brush off the losses emotionally, this would not have been a success. Even if you have more money, you did not win if you lost your mind in the process. Let us talk about the right mindset when you swing for the fences.

Project 7 contains simultaneous tasks using letters A, B, C, etc instead of numbered tasks. Remember that this means you may tackle each task in whatever order you prefer.

Task A: Understanding the "Swing for the Fences" Mentality

Swinging for the fences in investing means aiming for high returns by investing in assets with the potential to double or more in value over a brief period. This approach involves higher risk, and you must know that some of these investments will flop. The key is to recognize that you can take these risks because of the strong financial foundation you have built.

This is why you can afford to take risks now:

1. **Strong Emergency Fund:** You have a solid emergency fund in place, ensuring you can cover unexpected expenses without dipping into your investments.

2. **Insurance Coverage:** You have covered the big "what ifs" by insurance, protecting you from significant financial setbacks.

3. **High-Interest Debt Paid Off:** You have eliminated high-interest debt, which can erode wealth over time.

4. **Optimized Retirement Savings:** Your retirement savings are on track, with contributions maximizing available tax benefits.

5. **Non-Retirement Wealth:** You have diversified your investments and built wealth outside traditional retirement accounts.

Now that you are ready, let's delve into the diverse options for swinging for the fences. The following options are Higher-Risk, Higher-Reward Investment Options:

Task B: Concentrated Private Investments or Alternatives

Private investments or alternative assets include venture capital, private equity, hedge funds, and commodities. These investments often require significant capital and may have longer lock-up periods, but they offer the potential for substantial returns. There are medium-risk private and alternative investment options. A larger diversified fund is an example. That is more of a Project 6 investment. My investment in one restaurant start up was a swing for the fences decision. I would not consider that pool to be a diversified fund.

- **Venture Capital:** Investing in startups with high growth potential. While many startups fail, those that succeed can provide massive returns.

- **Private Equity:** Investing in private companies not listed on public exchanges. This often involves acquiring a stake in a company and later selling it at a higher value.

- **Hedge Funds:** Pooled investment funds that employ various strategies to earn active returns for their investors.

Task C: Concentrating into Fewer Stocks

Another strategy is to concentrate your investments in a smaller number of high-potential stocks. This approach is riskier than diversifying across many stocks but can lead to significant gains if the chosen companies perform well. A diversified stock portfolio is a Project 6 investment. Placing concentrated stock bets is swinging for the fences.

- **Growth Stocks:** Focus on companies expected to grow at an above-average rate compared to other companies.

- **Sector Bets:** Invest in sectors you believe will outperform the broader market, such as technology, healthcare, or renewable energy.

Task D: Concentrating into Digital Currencies

Digital currencies, such as Bitcoin, Ethereum, and other cryptocurrencies, have shown potential for exponential growth. However, they are also highly volatile and speculative. Let's think about real estate again for a moment for contrast. McDonalds has massive amounts of real estate. If the restaurant closed its doors, there would be a lot of real wealth to sell off and give to each shareholder/owner. Digital currencies don't have the same physical collateral. Without tangible assets, the value of an asset can go to zero. It doesn't mean it will, it just means it can. Bitcoin is the most well-known cryptocurrency, often referred to as digital gold. There are many other cryptocurrencies that can offer higher returns but come with increased risk. There are ways to invest in blockchain technology or a myriad of ancillary businesses. There are so many possibilities and so much volatility. This is why we didn't mention it until Project 7.

Task E: Speculative Real Estate or Land

Investing in speculative real estate or undeveloped land can yield high returns if the property value increases significantly.

- **Undeveloped Land:** Purchasing land in areas expected to grow can provide substantial appreciation over time.

- **Fix and Flip:** Buying, renovating, and selling properties for a profit.

Any real estate like apartment complexes in reasonable neighborhoods, long-term rental units/homes, and other standard real estate opportunities are part of Project 6. Do not interpret the entire real estate sector as swinging for the fences. Just as some stocks are steady, some real estate is steady. Some individual stock investments could be swinging for the fences and some real estate is.

Task F: Other High-Growth Potential Investments

Other investments with high growth potential can include collectibles (art, wine, cars), peer-to-peer lending, and investing in initial public offerings (IPOs).

- **Collectibles:** These can appreciate significantly over time but require knowledge of the market.

- **Peer-to-Peer Lending:** Lending money to individuals or small businesses through online platforms in exchange for interest payments.

- **IPOs:** Investing in companies when they first go public can offer high returns if the company succeeds.

Task G: Important Reminders

While these options have the potential for high returns, they come with significant risks. Always conduct thorough research and consider consulting with a financial advisor before making any high-risk investments. Keep in mind that your financial advisor is trained to help you reduce risk, not assume more. Remember, swinging for the fences is optional. You have already built a solid foundation through the previous projects, and your financial security does not depend on these high-risk strategies.

Task H: Have the right mentality.

Remember, you need to be willing to lose this money entirely. You will swing and miss with some of these investments. You may even feel like you are striking out. Project 7 is entirely optional. If you follow Projects 1 through 6, you will be successful. If you take the right mindset into your Project 7 investments, you will enjoy the experience. That is the key. Project 7 is not designed to help you mathematically. It has four purposes:

1. Create experiences through investing.
2. Help you realize not all investments are Project 6 ideas. Understanding the difference between Project 6 and Project 7 investments is key.
3. Provide a safer way to win big than playing the lottery
4. Develop relationships

If you think it will forever eat away at you if you lose a considerable sum of money, this is not for you.

Prosperity Project 7 Wrap Up

Project 7 is about giving you the knowledge and options to take calculated higher risks if you choose. By understanding the potential and risks of these high-reward investments, you can make informed decisions that align with your financial goals and risk tolerance. Whether or not you decide to swing for the fences, you now have the tools and knowledge to continue building your wealth and achieving financial freedom.

Prosperity Project 7 Checklist

- ☐ Task A: Understanding the "Swing for the Fences" Mentality
- ☐ Task B: Concentrated Private Investments or Alternatives
- ☐ Task C: Concentrating into Fewer Stocks
- ☐ Task D: Concentrating into Digital Currencies
- ☐ Task E: Speculative Real Estate or Land
- ☐ Task F: Other High-Growth Potential Investments
- ☐ Task G: Important Reminders
- ☐ Task H: Have the right mentality.

We have covered all the steps within the 7 Prosperity Projects. In the next chapter, I'll give you a summary of each project. Before the summary, I'm going to teach you how to get your head in the right place to make these decisions. I want these projects to do more for you than be interesting or engaging; I want them to change your life. You now have the steps. Next comes a decision-making framework to keep in mind throughout the journey.

Be Action Oriented

We have covered a comprehensive plan to help you achieve financial security, and it is worth recapping the key projects that form the foundation of this strategy. Before we dive deeper into the exact projects, let me make a simple comparison of these projects to a passenger train. It will help you understand the concept and remember the goal.

Get on the train!

These financial projects are like a moving train with eight railcars. Our goal is to reach the front of the train. The last railcar, or the caboose, is balancing your financial offense and defense. You must make enough money (play enough offense) to have the means to work through each project. You can slowly progress from the back of the train to the front as you complete the tasks within these projects. The next railcar in front of the caboose is Project 1, then Project 2, and so on.

Imagine you are at the station ready to board this financial-improvement train, but you do not know which railcar you are supposed to board. You have already plugged holes in the boat, you are getting free money, and you have started to make additional contributions in other retirement accounts. This means you are working on Project 3. Congratulations, you can board that train in railcar three.

Let's make a different assumption. Pretend you are struggling to pay down high-interest debt and you do not have enough life insurance. You should get in the caboose and work your way forward.

Every railcar in the train is connected and moving forward on the tracks. The important part is to just board the train. Congratulate yourself for being on the train. Those who sit at the station, wishing and wondering about the destination will be surprised and disappointed in their financial outcome. Those who get on the train and make some progress each year, find themselves at the front of the train without ever realizing it.

I am serious about that last part (the not realizing it part). Most everyone seems to have a nagging feeling of uncertainty about the strength of their own financial picture. Even those in the front of the train often feel like they are only halfway towards the front. I share that observation so you will understand you are doing better than you realize. You are not alone in your financial concerns. Give yourself some credit. You are at the end of a non-fiction financial self-improvement book with no real plot twists or true crime. Those who are in serious trouble rarely read a book like this.

The Prosperity Projects Recap

Prosperity Project 1: Plug the Holes in the Boat

We started by addressing the immediate and essential steps to protect your financial well-being: creating an emergency fund, securing appropriate insurance, establishing guardianship guidelines, and paying down high-interest debt. These steps are crucial to ensure you are prepared for life's unexpected challenges.

Prosperity Project 2: Get Free Money

Next, we explored ways to maximize your benefits by taking advantage of employer offerings such as HSA matching, retirement plan matching, and employee stock purchase plans. These are opportunities you should not miss, as they provide significant boosts to your savings.

Prosperity Project 3: Optimize Retirement Tax Benefits & Plans

We then focused on optimizing your retirement savings by carefully choosing the right accounts, assessing your current and future tax situations, and aligning your savings plan with your retirement goals.

Prosperity Project 4: Decide Who is in Charge

This project helps you understand foundational estate planning. It helps you protect the most important relationships in your life. You will dedicate time to documenting answers to emotionally tough questions about death, disability, assets, health, guardianship, and other key issues. It is heavy, but it is a labor of love.

Prosperity Project 5: Reduce Unwanted Debt

This project emphasizes effective debt management strategies, guiding you on how to prioritize and pay down debts to improve your financial health and free up resources for future investments.

Prosperity Project 6: Build Non-Retirement Wealth

We discussed the importance of diversifying your investments beyond retirement accounts. By investing in real estate, small businesses, and standard brokerage accounts, you can build wealth that offers flexibility and potential tax advantages.

Prosperity Project 7: Swing for the Fences

Finally, we encouraged you to take calculated risks with high-reward potential. Identifying and pursuing these opportunities can significantly boost your wealth and provide exciting prospects for your financial future.

Life Optimization as the Goal

Achieving financial security is about much more than accumulating wealth; it is about creating capacity in your life for peace, creativity, experiences, relationship building, and comfort. Financial security is not just a financial scorecard; it has the power to profoundly impact various aspects of your life. It can improve or even save marriages by reducing financial stress and fostering a collaborative approach to future planning. The financial stability you create today can lead to generational changes, offering your children better opportunities and a stronger foundation.

Beyond your relationships, financial security can improve your health. With the resources to afford time and care, you can prioritize your well-being and enjoy a higher quality of life. It is important to remember that this journey is a marathon, not a sprint. Do not be discouraged if progress seems slow at times. Focus on the next project and keep moving forward.

Thank you for allowing me to be a part of your financial journey. Remember, every step you take brings you closer to a more secure and fulfilling future. Keep working on your projects, stay committed, and watch as your efforts transform your financial landscape and enhance every aspect of your life.

Be Prosperous!

Zaccary Call

7 Prosperity Projects Worksheet

Use this list to keep track of your progress.

The Mindset

- ☐ Be action oriented.
- ☐ Get on the train!
- ☐ Life optimization as the goal

Prosperity Project 1: Plug the Holes in the Boat (pg. 31)

- ☐ Task A: Create an Emergency Fund
    - ○ Determining the Right Amount
    - ○ Steps to Build Your Emergency Fund
- ☐ Task B: Solve for "The Big What Ifs"
    - ○ Life Insurance
    - ○ Disability Insurance
    - ○ Guardianship
    - ○ Liability Insurance
- ☐ Task C: Pay Down High-Interest Debt

Prosperity Project 2: Get Free Money (pg. 47)

- ☐ Task 1: HSA Matching
- ☐ Task 2: Retirement Plan Matching
- ☐ Task 3: Employee Stock Purchase Plans (ESPP)

Prosperity Project 3: Automate Retirement Savings (pg. 59)

- ☐ Task 1: Determine How Much Money You Need to Save to Hit Your Retirement Goal
  - o Method 1: The Easy Table.
  - o Method 2: The Nerd's Manual Math
- ☐ Task 2: Review Your Current Income and Tax Situation vs. Retirement Tax Situation
- ☐ Task 3: Consider Whether You Will Try to Retire Before 59½ Years Old
- ☐ Task 4: Allocate Your Annual Savings to Various Tax Structures and Investments
- ☐ Task 5: Review Your Overall Savings Plan
- ☐ Task 6: Consider Investing in All Three Tax Types

Prosperity Project 4: Decide Who Is in Charge (pg. 91)

- ☐ Task 1: Foundational Estate Planning
  - ○ Trust – For death and disability
  - ○ Will – For death
  - ○ Power of Attorney – For disability or convenience
  - ○ Healthcare Directive – For disability and clarity
- ☐ Task 2: Create your Net Worth Statement
  - ○ List Your Assets
  - ○ List Your Debts
  - ○ Calculate Your Net Worth
- ☐ Task 3: Beneficiaries & Ownership Instructions
  - ○ Assign Beneficiary Designations
  - ○ Change Ownership to The Trust Now
  - ○ Use the Trust as the Beneficiary
  - ○ Create a Separate Document

Prosperity Project 5: Reduce Unwanted Debt (pg. 113)

- ☐ Task 1: Managing Reasonable Debt
- ☐ Task 2: Comparing Investment Returns with Debt Interest Rates
- ☐ Task 3: Debt Avalanche vs. Debt Snowball

Prosperity Project 6: Build Non-Retirement Wealth (pg. 123)

- ☐ Task 1: Understand Non-Retirement Wealth
- ☐ Task 2: Understand the Benefits of Investing Outside of IRAs and 401(k)s
    - o Flexibility
    - o Tax Management
    - o Diversification
- ☐ Task 3: Explore Non-Retirement Investment Options
    - o Standard Brokerage Accounts
    - o Real Estate
    - o Small Businesses
- ☐ Task 4: Implement a Non-Retirement Wealth Strategy

Prosperity Project 7: Swing for the Fences (pg. 137)

- ☐ Task A: Understanding the "Swing for the Fences" Mentality
- ☐ Task B: Concentrated Private Investments or Alternatives
- ☐ Task C: Concentrating into Fewer Stocks
- ☐ Task D: Concentrating into Digital Currencies
- ☐ Task E: Speculative Real Estate or Land
- ☐ Task F: Other High-Growth Potential Investments
- ☐ Task G: Important Reminders
- ☐ Task H: Have the right mentality

Zaccary Call

Learning More or Connecting with Me

Thank you for making it this far with me. It means a lot that you would consider these principles.

I am a leader of wealth advisors. My mission is to deliver superior financial planning to as many households as possible. I accomplish that by training advisors, helping clients, and sharing education publicly. This book is a part of the public education mission. I hope it has encouraged and empowered you to a better life through better money decisions.

If you have enjoyed this book, here are some additional financial education resources we have built that are available to you: My podcast called "The Financial Call". I am a regular guest on the Retirement Nerds YouTube Channel. I have written a retirement transition guide alongside Terri Flint called "Money & Mind." I regularly teach employer groups over webinars and in person. I am sure by the time you read this book, there will be other content available. Please look me up on Google or LinkedIn. I would love to hear ideas of how we could collaborate and use the 7 Prosperity Projects to better the lives of more people.

Made in the USA
Columbia, SC
05 May 2025

57571946R00091